"This is a delightful book. It contains the most complete repertoire on the theme of food in Luke's Gospel of which I know."

Hans-Josef Klauck, O.F.M.
Professor of New Testament and Early Christian Literature
The University of Chicago Divinity School, Chicago, Illinois

"Robert Karris writes with 'serious levity.' He has fashioned a 'meal' that provides enticing and nourishing food for thought, meat for good homilies, and staples for a life of Christian discipleship."

Marion C. Moeser, O.S.F.
Associate Professor of Sacred Scripture
Washington Theological Union, Washington, D.C.

Eating Your Way
Through Luke's Gospel

Eating Your Way
Through Luke's Gospel

Peace and all good—always.

Bob Karris

Robert J. Karris, O.F.M.

LITURGICAL PRESS
Collegeville, Minnesota

www.litpress.org

Cover design by David Manahan, O.S.B. Photo courtesy of PhotoSpin.

1	2	3	4	5	6	7	8

Library of Congress Cataloging-in-Publication Data

Karris, Robert J.
    Eating your way through Luke's Gospel / Robert J. Karris.
        p.   cm.
    Summary: "Considers the theme of food in Luke's Gospel; links issues of food in Luke with contemporary issues in church and society, as well as with contemporary sociological, cultural, and philosophical analyses of food"— Provided by publisher.
    Includes bibliographical references.
    ISBN-13: 978-0-8146-2121-9 (pbk. : alk. paper)
    ISBN-10: 0-8146-2121-X (pbk. : alk. paper)
    1. Food in the Bible. 2. Dinners and dining in the Bible. 3. Bible. N.T. Luke—Criticism, interpretation, etc. I. Title.

BS2595.6.D56K37 2006
226.4'06—dc22   2005010016

The Menu or Table of Contents

Introduction   1

Chapter 1   The Realia of Food and Drink during the Time
of Jesus and Luke   3

Chapter 2   The Theme of Food in Luke's Gospel   13

Chapter 3   Jesus, Glutton and Drunkard, Friend of
Toll Collectors and Sinners   25

Chapter 4   Jesus as Guest, Host, and Teacher at Meals   41

Chapter 5   Jesus' Petition for Food and Food Imagery in
Luke's Parables   55

Chapter 6   Trawling for the Theme of Food in the Gospels
of John, Mark, and Matthew   66

Chapter 7   Food and Women   82

Chapter 8   Eating Is a Serious and Dangerous, but Also
a Joyful Business   97

Selected Bibliography   104

Appendix: Correlation of Pages in the Book with Readings
of Luke's Gospel in Sunday Cycle C   107

Index   109

Introduction

I have fashioned this book for people doing continuing education in New Testament. Most of them have some background and want to learn more. They may be asking: "What's the latest?" or "How can I get a new angle on familiar materials?" Perhaps, adult education groups might also benefit from this work. If my readers are getting the drift that this is not a book for scholars, they've gotten my point. For teachers or those who might want additional resources I have added a section on Suggestions for Further Reading to each chapter. I conclude with a listing of books that I have found especially helpful.

My title indicates that I have written this book with serious levity. As my subject allows, I will add illustrations and anecdotes to get my point across. At the end of each chapter I provide some questions for further reflection. My final chapter will suggest how the theme of food in Luke may connect with contemporary issues.

This book has a dual origin. It first emerged from the oven of lively classroom discussion at Catholic Theological Union in Chicago and became a highly regarded chapter in my 1985 book *Luke: Artist and Theologian*. Since lots of new recipes on how to knead the theme of food in Luke's Gospel had hit the market since 1985, I decided to update and expand my materials for a 2004 summer session course at Graduate Theological Union, Berkeley, California. I thank the twelve students who participated in this course of continuing education: Machrina Blasdell, Sheila Brennan, Christine Gutleben, Jerry Holland, Jim Hopkins, Monica Lowy, Wayne Miraflor, Mary Morrison, Janet Reid, Michelle Stinson, Paul Watkins, and Patty Zatkin. I have learned much from our lively discussions from various faith traditions. I thank each one of them for making this a better book.

I dedicate this book to the president, dean, faculty, and staff of the Franciscan School of Theology, Berkeley, who over the years have generously opened their doors and hearts to this teacher, turned administrator, turned teacher again, turned researcher, turned teacher again. *Mille grazie!*

Unless otherwise noted, all biblical translations are from the *New American Bible.*

Chapter 1

The Realia of Food and Drink during the Time of Jesus and Luke

This first chapter deals with data that one rarely finds in contemporary commentaries or books on Luke's Gospel. Without a heavy dose of what I call "realia" or the "real things" we might quickly succumb to a lazy imagination. That is, we imagine or read into Luke's Gospel our contemporary notions and practices of food and drink and fail to try to imagine what it was really like back then. Take one simple example. Most of us relish pork whether as ribs, chops, hams, or bacon and would willy-nilly imagine Jesus and Luke sampling the same savory food. But Jesus and Luke were Jews who didn't eat pork. Those who have the money, motivation, and time can short-circuit their imaginations by traveling to an underprivileged country and partaking of its diet and thus learn firsthand what it was like for Jesus and Luke. Rice and beans may well be your daily fare. You might celebrate Sunday by adding one ounce of meat to your regular fare.

Let's continue to excite our imaginations and thereby shed a little of our cultural skins, so that we can read afresh what Luke says about Jesus and food. I indicate briefly some contrasts between our food culture and that of Jesus and Luke. After that I want to pick apart their menu and explore their wine cellar.

No hamburgers, hot dogs, brats, steaks, or ham for Jesus and Luke. They rarely ate meat and surely didn't eat pork.

We flock to the Friday fish fry. Fishermen Peter, Andrew, James, and John ate very little of the fish they caught, for they had to sell almost all their catch to pay their taxes.

Fewer and fewer foods are seasonal for us, as we can eat what we want when we want. Jesus and Luke eat table grapes in season and didn't enjoy red table grapes from Chile in January.

Jesus and Luke had no soft drinks or coffee or tea or beer or even bottled water. Boiled water and watered-down wine were the drinks of their day.

No ice cream. No sugar, whether real or artificial. Honey and fresh or dried fruit mollified their sweet tooth.

Two meals a day instead of our three squares with "midnight" snacks of pizza, popcorn, and potato chips.

White bread, made from the finest wheat, was for the rich. Coarse, cheap barley bread was for the poor. Those of us who still eat bread, which is full of carbs, prefer brown bread.

We eat on the run and graze, infrequently sitting together as a family. During those infrequent sit-down meals the sounds of cell phones and TV may be louder than our conversation together. Jesus, Luke, and their contemporaries knew of and participated in symposium meals, at which they reclined on couches and that were long and festive, featuring food and drink and lengthy conversation. No gulping and galloping at those meals.

A Leisurely Look at Food and Drink in Roman Palestine and in Luke's Environs

Perhaps it's good to begin with a sobering thought: During the time of Jesus and Luke, life expectancy at birth was about thirty years. Of course, diet was a big factor in a person's longevity. The rich had a better diet, while the poor person's diet was meager. When catastrophe or famine crashed the scene, death was near at hand for the poor. As one rabbinic source starkly puts it: "While the fat person becomes lean, the lean becomes dead."

After giving an overview of the diet of the rich and the poor in Roman Palestine, I will delve into the various food items in detail. What Gildas Hamel, a noted authority, says about Roman Palestine also applies to Luke's hometown:

> Wealthier people . . . were the only people regularly eating good meat, old wine, excellent bread, varied vegetables, fruit, and nuts. Most people ate bread or porridges made of barley, various cereals and legumes, or more rarely wheat. They supplemented them usually with salt and oil or olives, occasionally a strong sauce, honey, or sweet fruit juices. . . . They could not afford "noble" meat, except for festivities, and even then in small quantity. Greater poverty meant having a worse bread, full of bran and impurities, accompanied by salt and little oil. It also meant no meat and no vegetables, except roots and wild edible plants" (54–55).

Meat

Gildas Hamel has given the common wisdom regarding the consumption of meat in antiquity. Edwin Firmage agrees: "Regardless of the place or period in question, diets in antiquity were predominantly vegetarian. . . . Most people could afford to eat meat only on special occasions" (1120). Andrew Dalby forces us to put some nuance onto the common consensus, for he points to the Roman cook shops and the thriving trade in sausages, fat, and offal, and an established system of salting, and maintains: "In Rome . . . fresh meat was perhaps more prominent in the average weekly diet" (213). But it seems to me that these cook shops would not have been for the poor or of great interest to Luke, if he knew of them, for the meat on their menus mainly came from pigs. In brief, Jesus and Luke would have enjoyed lamb at annual Passover, for it was an exceptional treat.

Water

While most accounts take it for granted that people drank water, it should be emphasized that water was a major ingredient in the diet of Jesus and Luke. Peoples of old had learned, often through trial and error, that water should be boiled. So water was used in cooking, for drinking, and as a means of stretching and decreasing the strength of the wine consumed daily.

Wine

Wine was the main beverage, but generally mixed with three parts water. Magen Broshi has shown how plentiful wine presses were in Roman Palestine. For example, there were three hundred in Samaria alone. Broshi also estimates that the average daily consumption of wine was one liter. At this point I remind my readers that the second part of a symposium meal was mainly taken up with wine drinking and conversation, that Jesus was invited to many symposium meals in Luke, that Jesus was accused of being "a glutton and a drunkard" (Luke 7:34), that Jesus' final earthly meal in Luke 22 had cups of wine, and that the soldiers offered wine to the crucified Jesus (Luke 23:36).

Readers should not get the impression that all this wine was of superior quality. For example, the soldiers' wine was common stuff. Perhaps their wine was made from a recipe similar to that found in Cato's book "About Things Agricultural" no. 104:

> Wine for the slaves to drink through the winter. Pour into a vat 75 gallons of must, 15 gallons of sharp vinegar, 15 gallons of boiled must, 375 gallons of fresh water. Stir with a stick twice a day for five consecutive days. Then add 5 gallons of old sea water, cover the jar, and seal ten days later. This wine will last you until the summer solstice. Whatever is left over after the solstice will be a very sharp and excellent vinegar.

Incidentally, Cato fed his slaves on rough and dark bread, inferior olives, fish pickle, vinegar, and olive oil. Even those slaves, doing hard labor on the chain gang, got no meat, whether noble or otherwise.

Fish

Fish seems to dominate the first part of the story of Jesus in Luke, as Jesus calls fishermen to be his first disciples and moves about the Sea of Galilee in his ministry of mercy. As a matter of fact, Jesus causes Peter to catch so many fish that the catch threatens to sink not one, but two boats 26.5 feet long, 7.5 feet wide, and 4.5 feet deep that had a capacity in excess of one ton. It would seem that fish would be a major food item in Roman Palestine. Yet it was not, except in fish sauce. Megan Broshi comes to the startling conclusion that on average 1.4 ounces of fish were consumed per week per person. K. C. Hanson and Douglas E. Oakman remind us that the Sea of Galilee was a royal lake and that one had to pay to fish on it: "Fishing was controlled by the ruling elites. The local rulers . . . sold fishing rights to brokers . . . who in turn contracted with fishers. The fishers received capitalization along with fishing rights and were therefore indebted to the brokers . . . " (106). So most of the two boatfuls of fish went to the taxman.

People commonly consumed bread in a fish sauce, which made hard bread more palatable. Unfortunately I could not find a recipe for the fish sauce made at Magdala (in Greek, Tarichaeae, or "fish works") on the Sea of Galilee and three miles from Tiberias. Saint Mary of Magdala apparently never shared the recipe for her world famous fish sauce with anyone. Here is a less famous recipe: Various fish and innards of fish are to be mixed with plentiful salt and allowed to stand in the sun for about two months. Then pour the liquid off. The salty, fish liquid is called *garum*; the solid residue is called *allec*. While very flavorful, both stink to high heaven (see Dalby, 156). Dalby says that there is a close resemblance between these products and the fish sauce of modern Vietnam and Southeast Asia.

Bread

As we have seen already, poor people ate coarse, brown bread or barley bread, and the rich ate white bread. In his Fifth Satire,

Juvenal describes how the patron, Virro, treats his client, Trebius, at a banquet. The boss eats high off the hog whereas the subject barely gets a pig's foot. I quote the section about the different breads each is served:

> Trebius is given a bit of hard bread that he can scarcely break in two and bits of solid dough that have turned moldy, stuff into which no tooth can gain admittance. The patron and host, Virro, is served a delicate loaf of bread, white as snow and kneaded of the finest flour. If Trebius tries to take some of that bread from a nearby basket, the bossy servants tell him to put it down and learn the color of his bread.

If you're a brown-bread person, keep your hands off the white bread.

Each of the Gospels has the story of Jesus' multiplication of loaves. See Luke 9:10-17, for example. Although John is the only Gospel to mention that the loaves were made out of barley (6:9), it is no doubt true that this was the case in the miracles narrated in the other three Gospels. After all, barley bread was the bread of the people who followed Jesus. I have mused—in one of my lighter, humorous moments—whether there are two miracles here: the feeding of thousands from so little barley bread, and the fact that people didn't break their teeth on these hard loaves. Without the benefit of water or fish sauce or some relish these barley loaves were exceedingly hard and brutal on molars.

Symposium

When we think of a symposium, we most often think of a conference during which speakers will address various aspects of a theme, e.g., "A Symposium on Food." Our modern-day use of the word symposium captures just one dimension of what Jesus and Luke meant by a symposium. For Luke and Jesus a symposium was a meal, generally a festive one, at which the participants reclined, ate, drank wine, and conversed. In the strictest sense, the meal was first and was followed by the drinking of mixed wine and conversation. In Greek, symposium means "drinking with." Places of honor were generally on the middle couch of a three-couch or *triclinium* setup. On each of the three couches three people reclined. Thus, there would generally be nine people present. The Greco-Roman authors Lucian and Plutarch describe dignified women as present. Lucian places the women together by themselves on the left couch. In Luke's Gospel Jesus frequently eats at a symposium: with toll collector Levi (5:27-32); with Pharisee Simon (7:36-50); with other Pharisees (11:37-54); with still other Pharisees (14:1-24); with his male and female disciples (22:14-38). Many of the features we might find strange in Luke's accounts of Jesus' meals make sense in the setting of a literary symposium. For example, the strange fact that the woman sinner crashes the gate of the symposium in Luke 7:36-50 finds a ready parallel in "the uninvited guest" feature of the ancient symposium. Further, Lucian's *Symposium* satirizes the common practice of guests to squabble over who should get the choice couch at a symposium. Recall Luke 14:7-14.

Hospitality

The theme of hospitality holds hands with the theme of food in Luke's Gospel. The frequency with which the Lukan Jesus was invited to meals clearly indicates the high regard in which hospitality was held at his time. When the Samaritans were inhospitable to Jesus and his disciples as they journeyed to Jerusalem, Jesus forbade their destruction (Luke 9:52-56). Jesus the stranger blesses the hospitality of the two disciples journeying to Emmaus (24:13-35). There is a negative side to this theme of hospitality, though. Jesus wants the religious authorities to break open their guest lists and show hospitality to sinners, the poor, the blind, and the maimed (Luke 14:13, 21). As a matter of record, Jesus is accused of accepting hospitality from the wrong kind of people. He is "a friend of toll collectors and sinners" (7:34).

As the astute reader has begun to surmise, not everyone practiced generous hospitality at the time of Jesus and Luke. One of the reasons was that the householder could not be sure that the stranger was friend or foe. While Apuleius' *The Golden Ass* is a great romantic tale about the ill consequences of being too inquisitive (the hero is turned into an ass), its eleven chapters are chock full of stories of inhospitality, such as farmers unleashing attack dogs on a band of travelers who are seeking hospitality. I conclude this section with a summary of a tale from Book VIII of Ovid's *Metamorphoses*, which will highlight hospitality and a simple meal from "egg to apple" or, in our parlance, "from soup to nuts."

> After a thousand houses had barred their doors to the gods Jupiter and Mercury, Baucis and Philemon hospitably opened the doors of their humble cottage to them. This elderly couple prepare over the rekindled hearth a copper kettle for the cabbage from their garden that will be cooked along with a little bit of cherished smoked bacon. Conversation ensues, the guests' feet are washed, and they are bade to recline. The appetizers consist of low-grade olives, wild cherries preserved in the lees of some wine, endive, radishes, soft cheese, and eggs roasted in the coals of the hearth. All these foods were served in simple earthen dishes. Next comes the main course of the boiled cabbage with a bit of bacon. The wine of no great age is served in cups of beechwood coated on the inside with yellow wax. This was followed by the second course of nuts, figs, dried dates, plums, fragrant apples, and purple grapes just picked from the vine. In the center of the table was a comb of clear white honey. Besides all this, pleasant faces were at the board and lively and abounding goodwill. Since the wine did not run out, Baucis and Philemon realized that they were in the presence of the divine (Loeb Classical Library).

Note in this tale of exceptional hospitality that Baucis and Philemon serve their best, that little meat is served, that wine flows, and that egg comes first and apple last (in Latin: *ab ovo ad mala*).

Conclusion

I am a great fan of American classical music and often read the brochures that accompany the CDs. Sometimes I learn that a symphony or concerto has never been played before or is rarely played and thus has no or little performance history. The material I have presented in this chapter may be quite new, rarely heard in the classroom or from the pulpit. My goal has been simple. I want to excite our imaginations to read Jesus' story in Luke more from Jesus' and Luke's perspective on food than from our own.

Suggested Questions for Reflection

1. View Fellini's movie *Satyricon*, which humorously satirizes almost all the abuses that could possibly occur at a symposium. Contrast Fellini's meal with those of Jesus in Luke's Gospel.

2. On p. 33 of his *Food and Society in Classical Antiquity* (Cambridge: Cambridge University Press, 2001), Peter Garnsey writes: "In antiquity, food was power." In our day, is control of food still power, as squabbles over the composition of the food pyramid indicate? Who is exercising this power and why?

3. In the light of the information contained in this chapter, pick up Luke's Gospel and read chapter 16, verses 19-31. Have your eyes be opened to see this parable afresh?

Suggestions for Further Reading

Broshi, Magen. "The Diet of Palestine in the Roman Period: Introductory Notes" and "Wine in Ancient Palestine: Introductory Notes" in his *Bread, Wine, Walls and Scrolls*. Journal for the Study of the Pseudepigrapha Supplement Series 36. London/New York: Sheffield Academic Press, 2001, 121–43, 144–72.

Dalby, Andrew. *Food in the Ancient World from A to Z*. London/New York: Routledge, 2003.

Firmage, Edwin. "Zoology (Fauna)," *Anchor Bible Dictionary*. Volume 6. New York: Doubleday, 1992.

Hamel, Gildas. *Poverty and Charity in Roman Palestine, First Three Centuries*. Berkeley: University of California Press, 1990.

Hanson, K. C., and Douglas E. Oakman. *Palestine in the Time of Jesus*. Minneapolis: Fortress Press, 1998.

Ruscillo, Deborah. "When Gluttony Ruled!" *Archaeology* 54 (6) (2001) 20–7.

Chapter 2

The Theme of Food
in Luke's Gospel

Obstacles to Seeing the Theme of Food
in Luke's Gospel

In trying to appreciate food as a theme in Luke's Gospel, we may have serious obstacles to overcome. Those of us who are bound to the Lectionary face innumerable obstacles in appreciating Luke's Gospel during Cycle C of the church year. We have to wait until Lent, Holy Week, the Easter season, and the solemnities of Blessed Trinity and Corpus Christi are over before we begin to read Luke's Gospel, usually with chapter 4. Then we are fed bite-sized pieces of Luke's Gospel. Sometimes the Lectionary skips large slices of Luke's Gospel such as Jesus' cure of the Gerasene demoniac (8:26-39) that feature food, but seem too scandalous for Sunday congregations. In brief, the Lectionary throws up multiple roadblocks to a smooth reading of Luke's Gospel from beginning to end and may cause a severe case of Lectionary-itis.

My Roman Catholic readers may have special difficulty in appreciating the theme of food in Luke's Gospel because they have been socialized into seeing almost all occurrences of this motif as eucharistic. Let me give two quick examples. John the Baptist preaches that repentance must be shown by works of justice such as sharing food with the needy (3:11). Surely, John's preaching has nothing to do with the Eucharist, yet if our prescription glasses only allow us to see the Eucharist in Luke's text, we will miss this important passage and many more like it. While Jesus' prayer, "Give us each day our daily bread" (11:3), might well refer to the Eucharist, that is not its primary or only referent. To reduce Jesus' prayer to a prayer for daily Eucharist is to limit its scope and God's power. So I invite Roman Catholic readers to put aside their eucharistic template when they read Luke.

Even good practices such as daily meditative reading of a snippet of Luke's Gospel can erect obstacles to our smooth reading of Luke's Gospel in its entirety. We are like bumblebees, flitting from sweet flower to sweet flower to extract savory nectar, but never enjoying the beauty of the entire garden.

I recommend the following means of overcoming the three obstacles outlined above. Read Luke's Gospel from beginning to end in one sitting. Read with one goal in mind: to jot down all the passages that deal with food. You should find at least fifty references to food. I also wholeheartedly urge you to complete this bit of homework before you continue reading this chapter where I lay out the results of my reading. So no peeking at the answers until you've done your own work.

How to Detect a Theme

In her book on the theme of food in John's Gospel, Jane S. Webster has helpful materials on how to detect a theme. For our purposes, I reduce her five points to two: frequency and unexpectedness.

If my readers have truly done the homework I assigned, they may well smile at something I said years ago: In Luke's Gospel Jesus is either going to a meal, at a meal, or coming from a meal. References to food abound on almost every single page of Luke's Gospel. As one wag said: You can eat your way through Luke's Gospel. In brief, Luke frequently mentions food.

The second point, the unexpectedness of occurrences of food, may be harder for the ordinary reader to comprehend, for most readers are not familiar enough with the other three

Gospels to notice that a Lukan reference to food is unexpected. You see, most readers suffer from harmonizing-itis, as they throw all four Gospels into a blender and bolt down the end product of a single harmonized Gospel. Let me unwrap the notion of the unexpected a little by pointing out a few of the passages that Luke alone has. Luke is the only evangelist to have the following parables that feature food: The Prodigal Son whose return is celebrated with the fattened calf (15:11-32); The Rich Man who has daily sumptuous feasts and Lazarus, the poor beggar, who gets not even a crumb from the rich man (16:19-31). Luke alone of the evangelists tells the story of the two disciples on the way to Emmaus and how they recognized the stranger as the risen Lord at his breaking of the bread (24:13-35). Although food is not specifically mentioned in Luke 8:1-3 and 10:38-42, passages only found in Luke, the women who were serving Jesus were, among other things, engaged in providing food.

Even when Luke is not the only evangelist to tell a story, he often does something unexpected by situating the story around a meal. The most noticeable example is found in the materials that are found in both Luke 11:37-54 and Matthew 23:23-36. In both Luke and Matthew, Jesus takes the Pharisees and scribes to task, but it is only in Luke that Jesus' criticism occurs at a banquet. Luke 11:37 reads: "After he had spoken, a Pharisee invited him to dine at his home. He entered and reclined at table to see." Attentive readers can scour Matthew 23 for a similar meal setting and find none. It will take interested readers a little extra effort to notice the unexpected in my second example. It is only Luke that inserts the story of the disciples' dispute over precedence into his account of Jesus' last earthly meal. Compare Luke 22:24-30 with Mark 10:41-45 and with Matthew 20:24-28. In Mark and Matthew the disciples' contention over the first places occurs while Jesus is on the road to Jerusalem and not during a meal.

Indeed, food occurs frequently in Luke's Gospel and unexpectedly. Let's call it a theme.

The Big Picture of the Theme of Food in Luke's Gospel

Before noting the passages as they appear in sequence in Luke's Gospel, I offer some advance suggestions to my readers. As you jot down the references to food, try to arrange the materials into patterns; for example, animals as food; Jesus as guest at a banquet. Try your hand at giving these passages new headings. Headings such as "The Feeding of the Five Thousand" for Luke 9:10-17 have not come down from Mount Sinai and may lull us readers into thinking that we already know what the passage is all about. New headings, especially provocatively creative ones, may entice us to see a very familiar passage in a new light. To the extent possible, readers should try to locate the passage in the flow of Luke's Gospel. For example, ask whether the passage occurs in Luke's Introduction (Luke 1–4), Jesus' Galilean Ministry (4:16-9:50), Jesus' Journey to Jerusalem (9:51–19:27), Jesus' last days in Jerusalem (19:28–23:56), accounts of Jesus' resurrection (24:1-53). Might it be that references to food occur in all these major sections? The industrious reader might also want to see the connections between the theme of food and Luke's theme of the poor; for example, God gives food to a starving, poor, pagan widow (4:25).

Luke 1:15	The lips of John the Baptist will not taste wine or strong drink. See 7:33-34 and its contrasts between non-imbibing John and imbibing Jesus.
Luke 1:53	Mary's *Magnificat* proclaims that God will provide the hungry with food. See blessing for the hungry in 6:21 and woe against the full in 6:25.
Luke 2:7, 12, 16	Thrice Luke emphasizes that Jesus was laid in a manger as food for the world. Shepherds of sheep find Jesus in the manger.
Luke 2:24	Mary and Joseph offer the sacrifice of the poor, a pair of turtledoves or two young pigeons.

Luke 2:37	Anna, an aged widow, symbol of dependence upon God, fasts.
Luke 3:11	John the Baptist preaches that repentance is manifested by sharing food with the needy.
Luke 3:17	Unrepentant are chaff while repentant, wheat.
Luke 4:1-4	Jesus fasts as a sign of his dependence upon God for life.
Luke 4:25	God feeds a poor pagan widow caught in the throes of famine.
Luke 4:39	Simon's mother-in-law, healed by Jesus, waits on table *(diakonein)*.
Luke 5:1-11	Peter abandons the food of fish to follow Jesus, the source of true food.
Luke 5:14	Animal sacrifice for cleansing from leprosy (see Lev 14:10-32).
Luke 5:29-38	Dispute between Jesus and religious leaders over his eating habits, especially during Jesus' meal with Levi, toll collectors, and sinners.
Luke 6:1-5	The Sabbath, a day for celebrating life, and the question of eating.
Luke 6:21	God will provide food for the hungry.
Luke 6:25	A prophetic warning or woe for those who have full stomachs now.
Luke 6:43-46	Who are good fruit and who are bad fruit?
Luke 7:31-35	Criticism of John the Baptist for not drinking wine and eating only raw food, and of Jesus for being a glutton and a drunkard.
Luke 7:36-50	At this symposium meal, Jesus tangles with Simon about the significance of the acts a sinful woman lavishes upon him.
Luke 8:1-3	Women disciples share life *(diakonein)* with Jesus and fellow disciples.
Luke 8:11	Word of God that Jesus preaches gives life.
Luke 8:14	The pleasures of life, including those of the palate and gullet, can choke God's word from growing.

Luke 8:26-39	Jesus saves a man and causes a herd of hams, chops, and ribs to drown.
Luke 8:55	Jesus' mercy involves concern that people have something to eat.
Luke 9:3	Those who go on mission for Jesus take no food, but rely upon God for their sustenance.
Luke 9:10-17	Jesus is the center of attention as he gives abundant food to 5,000.
Luke 10:2	Harvest is a sign of mission.
Luke 10:7-8	Hospitality received: sharing of life, of food, and sharing of the Gospel are intimately connected.
Luke 10:33	A foreigner, a Samaritan, pours olive oil and wine on the wounds of the brutally beaten man.
Luke 10:38-42	Two women, a meal, discipleship, and sharing of life *(diakonein)*.
Luke 11:3	God is the source of our daily bread.
Luke 11:5-12	Food is for sharing life with friends and children.
Luke 11:27-29	Word of God supplies true nourishment.
Luke 11:37-54	At a banquet Jesus criticizes his host(s) for lack of justice. Sharing life is not a matter of external hygiene.
Luke 12:1	Teaching and lifestyle of the religious leaders is leaven that corrupts.
Luke 12:6	Sparrows are the cheapest food around.
Luke 12:13-34	Does one trust in God to provide life? One must share life with others through almsgiving (12:21, 33).
Luke 12:35-38	Reversal of expectations, as the Master serves *(diakonein)* the servants with food at table.
Luke 12:41-48	Disciples are to supply food to others.
Luke 13:6-9	Patience with the fig tree, so that it may produce food.
Luke 13:18-21	Mustard and white bread provide images of the kingdom of God.

Luke 13:26	Eating and drinking in Jesus' company is not enough.
Luke 13:29-30	The tables are turned as nonelect people from the four winds recline at God's eschatological table.
Luke 14:1-14	Don't squabble over the choice couch at a symposium banquet.
Luke 14:15-24	Invite poor, maimed, lame, and blind to recline at your banquet.
Luke 15:1-2	Religious leaders murmur over Jesus' table companions.
Luke 15:11-32	While much of this parable involves mercy and forgiveness, the aromas of the roasted fattened calf at a banquet rivet our attention.
Luke 16:7-8	Notes of indebtedness deal with olive oil and wheat.
Luke 16:19-31	Lazarus, a hungry, poor wretch, is a child of Abraham and has a choice spot at the heavenly banquet (16:22), while the well-fed rich man is outside.
Luke 17:7-10	In contrast to 12:35-38, servants must wait on tables.
Luke 18:12	Fasting gains a religious leader bragging rights over a toll collector.
Luke 19:7	People murmur about Jesus going to eat with a chief toll collector, Zacchaeus. See Levi in 5:27-32 and similar murmuring in 15:2.
Luke 20:9-18	Who will rightly tend the owner's vineyard?
Luke 20:46	Scribes use places of honor at banquets for self-exaltation.
Luke 21:34	Celebrating life to the point of intoxication avoids life.
Luke 22:1-38	Jesus does not eat his last earthly symposium meal with family, but with male and female disciples. Jesus is the one who serves at table *(diakonein)*.

Luke 23:36	One of the soldiers gives the crucified Jesus common wine to drink.
Luke 23:43	With his dying breath Jesus gives the food of life under the image of Paradise.
Luke 24:13-35	The giver of life is not dead. He continues to share life. God's kingdom is realized as Jesus eats with his disciples (see 22:18).
Luke 24:41-42	Disciples receive Jesus as a guest and feed him a piece of fish. He opens their eyes to see and share life.

In the next paragraphs, I lay a light burden on those readers who have little or no acquaintance with New Testament Greek. From the different words Luke uses, readers will glimpse Luke's rich vocabulary for food and reclining at table.

Luke uses a minimum of forty-five different words to express his theme of food; for example, drunkenness, fasting, and sumptuous daily dining. He also uses synonyms for food, some of which occur nowhere else in the New Testament. Taste these five samples that have Greek ingredients:

Luke 9:12	"provisions" (Greek: *episitismos*)
Luke 9:13	"food" *(brōma)*
Luke 12:23	"food" *(trophē)*
Luke 12:42	"portion of food" *(sitometrion)*
Luke 24:41	"anything to eat" *(brosimos)*

The *New American Bible and New Revised Standard Version* generally provide helpful translations of New Testament Greek, but are inconsistent or remiss in translating Luke's diverse vocabulary for participating at a symposium banquet. Too often they translate by "take a seat," Greek verbs that should be translated by "recline." Here are the cases in point:

Luke 5:29	"toll collectors were reclining at table" *(katakeimenoi)*
Luke 7:36	"Jesus reclined at table" *(kateklithē)*
Luke 7:49	"those reclining with him" *(synanakeimenoi)*

Luke 9:14	"Have them recline" *(kateklinate)*
Luke 9:15	"All reclined" *(kateklinan)*
Luke 11:37	"Jesus reclined at table" *(anepesen)*
Luke 12:37	"Make them recline at table" *(anaklinei)*
Luke 13:29	the non-elect "will recline at table" *(anaklithēsontai)* in God's kingdom
Luke 14:10	"those reclining at table with you" *(synanakeimenōn)*
Luke 22:14	"the apostles reclined at table with him" *(anepesen)*
Luke 22:27	Who is greater: the one reclining at table *(anakeimonos)* or the one serving?
Luke 24:30	"When the stranger was reclining at table with them" *(kataklithēnai)*

Even through the haze of these Greek terms, readers can catch a glimpse of how versatile Luke is in his use of food imagery and in his use of words for reclining at table for a banquet or symposium meal.

Animals

Before I scamper into the next chapter to treat Jesus eating with sinners, I call the attention of my readers to what may be subthemes of food in Luke. In their careful reading of all twenty-four chapters of Luke's Gospel, very alert readers may have noticed how frequently Luke mentions animals. Animals are a subtheme of food, it seems. Perhaps, those iconographers who depicted Luke with a sacrificial ox at his side were right on the money, for Luke has a thing about animals. In contemporary scholarly literature, Luke's focus on animals is nary given a shrug of the shoulders. A chapter in Joseph Grassi's *Peace on Earth* is the rare exception. In ages past, scholars such as St. Bonaventure (d. 1274) gave much attention to the significance of animals in Luke. In an attempt to jump-start us into noting the frequency with which Luke mentions animals I single out the following passages:

Luke 2:8	Shepherds who tend sheep, useful for wool and food.
Luke 2:24	Jesus' parents offer the food of the poor as a sacrifice: a pair of turtledoves.
Luke 3:22	Holy Spirit appears as a dove.
Luke 5:1–11	Jesus calls fishermen away from their livelihood of catching fish for food.
Luke 8:5	Birds of the sky eat up seed that is sown.
Luke 8:32	Herd of many pigs was nearby.
Luke 9:58	Foxes have dens, and birds of the sky have nests.
Luke 10:11	Power to tread upon serpents and scorpions.
Luke 10:34	The Samaritan stranger lifted the wounded man up on his own animal.
Luke 11:11–12	What father among you would hand his son a snake when he asks for a fish? Or hand him a scorpion when he asks for an egg?
Luke 12:6	Five sparrows sold for two small coins.
Luke 12:24	Notice the ravens: they do not sow or reap . . .
Luke 13:1	Galileans whose blood Pilate had mingled with that of their sacrifices.
Luke 13:19	Birds of the sky dwell in the branches of the mustard seed.
Luke 13:32	Jesus calls Herod a fox.
Luke 13:34	How many times I (Jesus) yearned to gather your children together as a hen gathers her brood under her wings.
Luke 14:19	I have purchased five yoke of oxen and am on my way to evaluate them.
Luke 15:4	One of 100 sheep is lost.
Luke 15:15	Prodigal Son tends hogs.
Luke 15:23	Slaughter the fattened calf (see also 15:27, 30).
Luke 15:29	You never even gave me a kid goat to celebrate with my friends.
Luke 16:21	The unclean dogs lick the wounds of the miserable poor man.
Luke 17:7	Servant plowing or tending sheep.

Luke 17:37	Where the body is, there also will the vultures gather.
Luke 18:25	Easier for a camel to pass through the eye of a needle.
Luke 19:30-40	Jesus enters Jerusalem on a colt upon which no one has yet ridden.
Luke 19:45-46	Cleansing of the Temple does not explicitly mention animals, but they were sold there.
Luke 22:7	Day for sacrificing the Passover lamb.
Luke 22:34	Before the cock crows, you will deny me thrice.
Luke 22:60-61	Cock crows, and Peter remembers.
Luke 24:42	Disciples give the risen Jesus a piece of cooked fish.

At first blush, it seems that some of the animals mentioned in Luke's Gospel would not regularly serve as human food: dog, raven, fox, camel, scorpion, snake. Jewish Jesus and Luke would not eat pork. But chicken, fish, lamb, kid goat, and fattened calf would find ready and happy eaters.

Conclusion

Now that we have seen the big picture of the theme of food in Luke's Gospel, we are on the brink of breaking this gargantuan theme down into more manageable morsels. A key question to ask is: Through its theme of food, what does a particular passage say about God? What does it say about Jesus?

Suggested Questions for Reflection

1. Are you really convinced that food is a theme in Luke's Gospel? Are some passages that I have listed above more convincing than others?

2. Can you think of other books in the Bible where food is a major theme? Genesis with the Garden of Eden, and Joseph, Egypt's food czar? Exodus with Passover and manna in the

desert? Belshazzar's great banquet with the mysterious words, Mene, Tekel, Peres, and Daniel's interpretation? The account in 1 Maccabees of Antiochus' persecution of the Jews who would not eat unclean food such as pork?

3. Do your favorite TV programs, movies, or novels use food and drink as a theme? I enjoy reading mysteries. One of my favorite authors is Andrea Camilleri whose Inspector Montalbano works in Sicily and celebrates life by enjoying marvelous meals before or after catching a crook.

Suggestions for Further Reading

Karris, Robert J. *Luke: Artist and Theologian.* New York: Paulist Press, 1985, 47–78. This chapter updates the materials found on pages 47–52 in my earlier work.

Grassi, Joseph. "Jesus' Compassion for Animals: A First Step Toward a Nonviolent World," in his *Peace on Earth: Roots and Practices from Luke's Gospel.* Collegeville: Liturgical Press, 2004, 147–57.

St. Bonaventure's Commentary on Luke's Gospel, Chapters 1–8, Chapters 9–16, Chapters 17–24. With an Introduction, Translation, and Notes by Robert J. Karris. Works of St. Bonaventure VIII/1–3; St. Bonaventure, NY: Franciscan Institute Publications, 2001, 2003, and 2004.

Ryken, Leland, and others, eds. *Dictionary of Biblical Imagery.* Downers Grove, IL: InterVarsity Press, 1998.

Webster, Jane S. *Ingesting Jesus: Eating and Drinking in the Gospel of John.* Society of Biblical Literature Academia Biblica 6; Atlanta: Society of Biblical Literature, 2003, 8–12.

Chapter 3

Jesus, Glutton and Drunkard, Friend of Toll Collectors and Sinners

In this chapter I group together a number of passages around the topic of Jesus' association with sinners and toll collectors. After exploring the meaning of Luke 7:34, a summary passage, I will focus on Jesus' relationship with the following sinners: Peter, Levi, an unnamed woman sinner, Zacchaeus, and the Good Thief. Some might complain that I am restricting the menu too much with these few passages. I respond that although I would like to display a full smorgasbord of passages, I have been advised that five items at a time aids good digestion and assimilation. Others will surely complain, as they carefully read my table of contents, that in my next chapter some of these same passages will surface as tasty leftovers, but leftovers nonetheless. To those who might complain on these two scores, I offer the following sop: After you have seen how I organize Luke's food passages, you can decide for yourself whether I've made them appetizing and appealing. If my arrangement is not satisfying, my readers can reorganize and rearrange Luke's food passages to their hearts' content. Someone had to get the ball rolling.

Jesus Loves Eating and Drinking and Loves to Be with Outcasts—Luke 7:34

I translate Luke 7:34: "I have come eating and drinking, and you say: Look at him, a glutton and a drunkard, the friend of toll collectors and sinners." Contrary to what Leif E. Vaage maintains, this verse does not depict reality as if Jesus were an "omnivorous sot," living in "the fog of a hangover that envelopes the fearless feaster." Luke 7:34 is a slur, similar to those that shriek through our media during a dirty political campaign. That is the meaning of "You say." But as we well know, slurs have some truth behind them, as in the dictum: "Where there's smoke, there's fire." So let's follow the smoke behind the words: glutton and drunkard, friend, toll collectors, sinners.

Scholars present two Old Testament passages to interpret "glutton and drunkard." Each sheds some light. The first is Deuteronomy 21:18-21:

> If a man has a stubborn and unruly son who will not listen to his father and mother, and will not obey them even though they chastise him, his father and mother shall have him apprehended and brought out to the elders at the gate of his home city, where they shall say to those city elders, "this son of ours is a stubborn and unruly fellow who will not listen to us; he is a glutton and a drunkard." Then all his fellow citizens shall stone him to death. Thus shall you purge the evil from your midst, and all Israel, on hearing of it, shall fear.

Deuteronomy 21:18-21 helps interpret Luke 7:34 because Jesus' ways of eating and drinking did go against the social and religious norms of his society. I note that the Greek of Luke 7:34 *(phagos kai oinopotēs)* is not the same as the Greek of Deuteronomy 21:20 *(symbolokopon oinophlygei)*.

Another OT passage is Proverbs 23:20-21, which contrasts the ways of the wise with those of the foolish. The translation of the Hebrew is: "Consort not with drunkards, nor with those who eat meat to excess. For the drunkard and the glutton come to poverty, and torpor clothes a man in rags." The Greek word behind "drunkard" *(oinopotēs)* in Proverbs 23:20 is the same as that in Luke 7:34. Unfortunately, the parallel stops there, for the Greek of Proverbs 23:21 should be translated "drunkard and fornicator." In any case, the contrast in Proverbs 23:20-21 is between what a wise person and what a fool would do. The accusation against Jesus is that in his eating and drinking (and in his selection of table companions) he is not acting like a wise person, but like a fool.

Deuteronomy 21:18-21 and Proverbs 23:20-21 have opened our eyes to see how Jesus' conduct of eating and drinking might have been interpreted in a society of religious Jews. We now add to our first impressions by exploring the meaning of the next words, "friend of toll collectors and sinners."

Friend

I discuss this key word from two angles. The Old Testament Wisdom Literature has much to say about friends. Sirach 11:29–14:19, for example, has much sage counsel about the persons with whom one should strike up a friendship and those whose company one should avoid. Sirach 13:13-19 advises:

> Be on your guard and take care never to accompany men of violence. Every living thing loves its own kind, every man a man like himself. Every being is drawn to its own kind; with his own kind every man associates. Is a wolf ever allied with a lamb? So it is with the sinner and the just. Can there be peace between the hyena and the dog? Or between the rich and the poor can there be peace? Lion's prey are the wild asses of the desert; so too the poor are feeding grounds for the rich. A proud man abhors lowliness; so does the rich man abhor the poor (NAB).

According to this wisdom teaching, Jesus should not be making friends with those who are not his own kind, that is, with toll collectors and sinners. Jesus' conduct is scandalous.

Luke builds upon Jesus' friendship with society's outcasts and describes it from the Greco-Roman viewpoint that friends have all things in common. Acts 2:44 describes the first believers, from all walks of life, as friends: "All who believed were together and had all things in common." In a similar fashion Acts 4:32 says: "The community of believers was of one heart and mind, and no one claimed that any of his possessions was his own, but they had everything in common." As Alan C. Mitchell says: "Christians can become friends regardless of culturally promoted and accepted status divisions and without the need to give with an eye to a return" (240). In acting in such a friendly manner toward one another, the first Christians were imitating Jesus who broke down the barrier and crossed the boundary separating those of different social and religious status. Further, the Greek word behind friend is *philos*, the same Greek word that begins Phil-adelphia. It is both active and passive: Jesus loves sinners and toll collectors and is loved by them in return.

In summary, from either an OT or a Greco-Roman perspective, Jesus should not have befriended toll collectors and sinners. They are not his kind.

Toll Collectors

We can deal much more briefly with the toll collectors. In general, those involved with collecting taxes in antiquity were not held in high regard. In Roman Palestine the toll collectors are mainly involved with collecting indirect taxes such as those levied on the transport of goods. If you want a rough, contemporary example, just think of our toll roads, toll bridges, and tollbooths. Both Levi (Luke 5:27-32) and Zacchaeus (19:1-10) had strategic places for collecting such taxes. Ancient toll collectors were often greedy and dishonest, two sins that contributed to their disdain among the populace. Jesus befriends such distasteful people.

Let me make clear a point that has just surfaced with the names of toll collectors Levi and Zacchaeus and will become clearer in what follows. Toll collectors occur frequently in Luke's Gospel and are generally favorably disposed to conversion. See John the Baptist's preaching in Luke 3:12-13: "Even toll collectors came to be baptized and they said to John, 'Teacher, what should we do?' He answered them, 'Stop collecting more than what is prescribed.'" In an aside, Luke comments: "All the people who listened, including the toll collectors, and who were baptized with the baptism of John, acknowledged the righteousness of God; but the Pharisees and scholars of the law, who were not baptized by him, rejected the plan of God for themselves" (7:29-30). Recall the parable of the Pharisee and the toll collector in Luke 18:9-14. The toll collector acknowledges his sin and asks for God's mercy.

Sinners

In its basic meaning, "a sinner" is one who does not keep the Jewish Law and is usually contrasted with "the righteous," who do keep the Law. Psalm 1:1-2 says: "Happy those who do not follow the counsel of the wicked. Nor go the way of sinners, nor sit in company with scoffers. Rather, the law of the Lord is their joy; God's law they study day and night." Sirach 41:8 reads: "Woe to you, O sinful men, who forsake the law of the Most High." Those who keep the Law may well think that sinners occupy a lower social-religious status and should actually be excluded from their company. Put another way, the righteous would not cultivate the friendship of sinners or recline at table with them. Jesus' Parable of the Pharisee and the Toll Collector is a parade example of the conduct of a righteous one and a sinner (18:9-14).

As we work our way through Luke's food imagery in this chapter, we will be amazed to see how often the word "sinner" or its equivalent turns up in a food context. Peter the fisherman confesses that he is "a sinful man" (Luke 5:8). Twice in Luke 5:27-32 the word "sinner" is spoken at Levi's table. Luke 7:36-50 mentions "sinner" twice and "sins" two times as Luke recounts the story of Simon the Pharisee hosting Jesus. In the three parables (lost sheep, coin, and son) that comprise Luke 15, "sinners" and "sin" pop up six times. Finally, Zacchaeus, a chief toll collector, is called "a sinner" as he prepares to spread a table for Jesus. We might well ask the question: Are those who complain that Jesus is eating with sinners and toll collectors sinners themselves and in need of repentance?

I conclude my discussion of Luke 7:34 by reiterating my point that this is a summary statement of Jesus' conduct. Toll collectors and sinners love Jesus, and he loves them. Jesus loves life and enjoys eating and drinking with men and women, be they sinners or not.

Peter the Sinner—Luke 5:1-11; 22:31-34, 54-62; 24:34-42

In the sacristy of St. Anthony's Chapel in Kennebunkport, Maine, there is a large stained-glass window of St. Peter. As you look Peter in the eye, you are stunned by his majesty and the gold of the keys of the kingdom he holds in his hands. As your eye roams over this captivatingly beautiful window, you notice that just to the right of Peter's shoulder there is a rooster crowing. Peter was not only a fisherman, was not only called to catch men and women for Christ, but he was also a sinner.

Although Luke introduces Peter already in Luke 4:38-39, I start with Jesus' call of Peter in 5:1-11. In chapter 1, I noted that on average only 1.4 ounces of fish were consumed weekly per person in Roman Palestine. Further, I mentioned the heavy taxes that Peter had to pay to fish on the royal Sea of Galilee. Finally, from archaeological finds we surmise that each of Peter's two boats was 26.5 feet long, 7.5 feet wide, and 4.5 feet deep; each had a capacity of one ton. In brief, this is a fish-food story.

For our present purposes Luke 5:8 is key: "When Peter saw this (the huge catch of fish), he fell at the knees of Jesus and said: 'Depart from me, Lord, for I am a sinful man.'" Because of the astonishingly large catch of fish made at Jesus' mere command, Peter realizes that he is in the presence of the divine. Hence, his use of the title "Lord." As we know from OT passages such as the call of Isaiah, human beings are almost overwhelmed with a sense of their sinfulness in the presence of the divine. Isaiah pleads: "Woe is me, I am doomed! For I am a man of unclean lips, living among a people of unclean lips; yet my eyes have seen the King, the Lord of hosts!" After one of the seraphim had touched Isaiah's mouth with a burning ember, he said: "See. Now that this has touched your lips, your wickedness is removed, your sin purged" (Isa 6:1-7). Perhaps Jesus' call of Peter is far less dramatic. I paraphrase Luke 5:9: "Do not be fearful at this display of divine power. From now on, like good teachers, you will be catching women and men hook, line, and sinker for the kingdom of God."

I jump ahead in the Gospel story to two passages in Luke 22 where Peter appears. During Jesus' last earthly meal with his male and female disciples, he predicts Peter's denial. Would it be too bold to say that Jesus is predicting the sin of Peter, who is eating and drinking with him at this solemn moment? Here is the text:

> Simon, Simon, behold Satan has demanded to sift all of you like wheat, but I have prayed that your own faith may not fail; and once you have turned back, you must strengthen your brothers. He said to him: "Lord, I am prepared to go to prison and to die with you." But he replied, "I tell you, Peter, before the cock crows this day, you will deny three times that you know me."

Imbedded within this prediction of Peter's denial is one of the few New Testament texts about the power of Jesus' intercessory prayer: "I have prayed that your own faith may not fail." As a result of Jesus' powerful prayer, Peter's faith does not fail.

Luke 22:54-62 contrasts the steadfastness of Jesus and the cowardice of Peter. Luke 22:60-62 are vital:

> But Peter said, "My friend, I do not know what you are talking about." Just as he was saying this, the cock crowed, and the Lord turned and looked at Peter, and Peter remembered the word of the Lord, how he had said to him, "Before the cock crows today, you will deny me three times." He went out and began to weep bitterly.

Peter, all so human in the Gospel tradition, realizes the sin of his denial and weeps over it.

The story of Peter the sinner is not complete, however, without Luke 24:34-42. Luke 24:34 simply states: "The Lord has truly been raised and has appeared to Simon." It seems likely that the risen Lord did not appear to Simon to pass the time of day. Forgiveness and rehabilitation would have been the main components of this appearance, if John 21:15-17 is any indication. Finally, don't forget to look at 24:42: Jesus, perhaps not surprisingly, eats fish with his male and female disciples, Peter included.

It seems that food is a dominant force in Luke's story of Peter. Peter is called while providing food. Peter sins while breaking bread with Jesus. The risen Lord forgives Peter and eats with him. I once invited to supper someone who had been grievously offended at a decision made by my predecessor in office. He accepted. No actual words of reconciliation were spoken, but forgiveness was in the air and on the table and in our demeanor.

Toll Collector Levi Hosts a Lavish Banquet for Jesus— Luke 5:27-32

With the story of Jesus' table fellowship with toll collector Levi (Luke 5:27-32), we reach a critical point in our investigation as we begin to ask questions about Luke's presentation of Jesus. Are Jesus' meals with outcasts just an expression of his outstanding humanity and generosity of spirit or do they say more about Jesus and about the God he preaches? That is, are Jesus' meals with sinners "acted parables" of the kingdom of God? The famous German NT scholar Joachim Jeremias thought so. What he wrote of "the historical Jesus" applies equally well to Luke's portrayal of Jesus:

> In the East, even today, to invite a person to a meal was an honor. It was an offer of peace, trust, brotherhood, and forgive-

ness. In short, sharing a table meant sharing life. In Judaism in particular, table fellowship means fellowship before God, for the eating of a piece of broken bread by everyone who shares in a meal brings out the fact that they all have a share in the blessing which the master of the house had spoken over the unbroken bread. Thus Jesus' meals with the toll collectors and sinners, too, are not only events on a social level, not only an expression of his unusual humanity and social generosity and his sympathy with those who were despised, but had an even deeper significance. They are an expression of the mission and message of Jesus (Mark 2:17), eschatological meals, anticipatory celebrations of the feast in the end time (Luke 13:28-29; Matt 8:11-12), in which the community of the saints is already being represented (Mark 2:19). The inclusion of sinners in the community of salvation, achieved in table fellowship, is the most meaningful expression of the message of the redeeming love of God" (*New Testament Theology: The Proclamation of Jesus*. New York: Scribner's, 1971, 115–6, with stylistic modifications).

Perhaps, we can get at some of the meaning of this initial banquet scene in Luke by peeling back some of its strange layers. If Levi has truly left all things, how can he throw a gigantic banquet for Jesus? Can you imagine all the people reclining at the same table or even at a single table in Levi's house? Surely, there are too many for a *triclinium* or three-couch arrangement with three on each couch. First, there's Levi and Jesus. Then the text notes a great crowd of toll collectors and others. There are also Pharisees and their scribes who would not want to be at table with toll collectors. Then, too, the disciples, whom Jesus has just called, are present. It is they who have to answer the question of why they are eating and drinking with toll collectors and sinners when Jesus was the one invited to eat and drink with them. Furthermore, earlier in his narrative Luke had not mentioned that Jesus' disciples ate with toll collectors and sinners. Moreover, the Pharisees and their scribes add invective to their question by referring not to "toll collectors and others," but to "toll collectors and sinners." Finally, Jesus' disciples do not answer the question the Pharisees and their scribes put to them, but Jesus does. Jesus' answer may be ironic. Physicians help those who confess that they are sick. However, they can't help those who think they are well, but are really sick. If the world is divided into the righteous and the sinners, Jesus has come for the sinner, but perhaps the righteous are self-righteous and also need Jesus' help and should repent.

The strange features of this story tell me that Luke has tailored Jesus' call of Levi to his theological purposes. Not only Jesus, but also his disciples are going to get into trouble with the authorities because of their eating and drinking practices. These authorities will be the food police who will be ever vigilant to pounce on any violation of food protocols that Jesus commits. Also, this passage, so early in Luke's Gospel, is a preview of coming attractions, for Luke will present Jesus in controversy with the religious leaders during three more meals (7:36-50; 11:37-54; 14:1-24).

We can look at Jesus' call of Levi from yet another angle. It is the second of the five controversy stories between Jesus and the Pharisees that Luke presents in Luke 5:17–6:11. Luke 5:17-26 deals with Jesus' power to forgive sins. Luke 5:27-32 concerns Jesus' eating and drinking with toll collectors and sinners. Luke 5:33-39 picks up the question of why the disciples of John the Baptist and the Pharisees fast while Jesus' disciples eat and drink. In Luke 6:1-5 Jesus defends his disciples who are eating on the Sabbath. In Luke 6:6-10 Jesus does good on a Sabbath by restoring a man's withered right hand. Luke concludes these stories with: "But they (the scribes and the Pharisees) became enraged and discussed together what they might do to Jesus" (6:11). Each of these controversies, in its own way, anticipates future stories in Luke's Gospel. For example, Jesus' power to forgive sins (5:17-26) will resurface in the next story we consider (7:36-50).

In brief, Luke's Jesus, upon whom the Spirit of the Lord rests (4:18), calls despised people such as toll collectors to follow him and enjoys reclining at table in their company.

A Woman, Who Is a Sinner, Lavishes Gracious Hospitality on Jesus—Luke 7:36-50

I will lavish special consideration upon this passage in my next chapter. My purpose here is to clear out some brambles that might hinder our subsequent interpretation.

Our first crop of brambles flourishes around the name of the woman in this passage. Despite what *The Da Vinci Code* and thousands of years of Christian tradition maintain, the woman in this passage is not Mary Magdalene. Readers who persist in this error can read this passage forwards and backwards, in English translations and in the original Greek. Nowhere does this passage name the woman.

The second bunch of brambles is nourished by the erroneous viewpoint that the woman in this passage is a sinner because she was a harlot. Nowhere does this passage specify her sin. She might have poisoned her adulterous husband or she might have been a nefarious gossip. Nor does this passage give the woman's age. She might have been a grandmother whose sin was avarice.

A third bundle of brambles is related to the second bunch and is fed by our tendency to harmonize Luke 7:36-50 with the parallel accounts of a woman's anointing in Mark 14:3-9, Matthew 26:6-13, and John 12:1-10. While all four accounts situate the anointing at a meal, Luke is the only evangelist who does not narrate a disciple's outrage at the waste and does not question why the money for this ointment wasn't given to the poor. Further, in John the woman who anoints Jesus is Mary, the sister of Lazarus. In Mark and Matthew the woman is unnamed. *But most important is the fact that neither Mark nor Matthew nor John say that the woman was a sinner.* That is, it is only Luke who says that the woman who anointed Jesus was a sinner.

If we look back at the five controversy stories of Luke 5:17–6:11, we may recall that the first controversy dealt with Jesus' power to forgive a man's sins. In 7:36-50 Luke balances Jesus' previous forgiveness of a man's sins with his forgiveness of a woman's sins. In both cases a similar question surfaces: "Who but God alone can forgive sins?" (5:21) and "Who is this who even forgives sins?" (7:49). Indeed, Luke continues to paint his picture of Jesus.

Zacchaeus, Wealthy Chief Toll Collector, Hosts Jesus— Luke 19:1-10

I begin by noting a few similarities and dissimilarities between this story and Jesus' earlier dealing with the toll collector Levi (5:27-32). Early in his Galilean ministry Jesus called Levi, who, in turn, hosted a big supper for Jesus, his disciples, and toll collectors and others. In 19:1-10 Jesus, at the end of his journey to Jerusalem, encounters his final toll collector, Zacchaeus, who is a chief toll collector and wealthy. The Pharisees and their scribes criticized Jesus' disciples, and through them Jesus, for eating and drinking with toll collectors and sinners. The people criticize Jesus for staying with Zacchaeus, a sinner (19:7). Whereas Levi invited Jesus into his house for a banquet, Jesus invites himself to Zacchaeus's house for a meal. Although no explicit mention is made of food in 19:7, it surely is to be understood that Jesus and Zacchaeus broke bread together.

The more immediate context of Luke 19:1-10 tells us more of Zacchaeus's significance in Luke's eyes. Zacchaeus, as he humiliates himself by climbing a tree, is like the vulnerable little children who image those to whom the kingdom of God belongs (18:15-17). In giving 50 percent of his possessions to the poor and in providing fourfold restitution, Zacchaeus is positively contrasted with a fellow rich official who cannot say goodbye to his money (18:18-23). To the extent possible, Zacchaeus, through his forsaking of possessions for the needy, imitates the generosity of Jesus who will undergo the cross and experience the resurrection (18:31-34). The blind man (18:35-43) and Zacchaeus have many things in common. For example, both are beggars, both want to see Jesus, and both withstand the obstacles of the crowd to accomplish their goal. Through the above literary connections,

Luke is showing that Zacchaeus, although a sinner, is well disposed to receive Jesus' invitation to come to Zacchaeus's house.

It behooves us to tarry just a bit on Luke 19:9-10: "And Jesus said to him: 'Today salvation has come to this house because this man too is a descendant of Abraham.' For I have come to seek and to save what was lost." Seeking, finding, and saving what was lost was a common thread through the three parables of Luke 15, as the shepherd, the woman, and the father sought what was lost and rejoiced when it was found. Time and space limitations prevent me from developing at length Luke's motif of who is a child or descendant of Abraham. It may be sufficient to point to three passages. In his preaching, John the Baptist warned the Jewish people that actions, and not just lineage, determined who is a child of Abraham: "Produce good fruits as evidence of your repentance, and do not begin to say to yourselves, 'we have Abraham as our father,' for I tell you, God can raise up children of Abraham from these stones" (3:8). A woman who had been crippled for eighteen years and is cured by Jesus on a Sabbath is "a daughter of Abraham" (13:10-17). The figure of Abraham occurs seven times in the Parable of the Rich Man and Lazarus (16:19-31). It is the poor beggar Lazarus who occupies the choice couch next to Abraham at the eternal banquet.

In brief, we find Luke describing Jesus' happy association with sinners in yet another major portion of his Gospel. Jesus even goes out of his way to befriend them, as is fitting for someone who was accused of being "the friend of toll collectors and sinners."

The Good Thief Steals Paradise—Luke 23:39-43

This remarkable passage has been called "The Gospel within the Gospel," for it captures so well God's mercy revealed in Jesus. Unfortunately, most people may just have a fleeting acquaintance with it, for it occurs in the Lectionary once every three years, and then as part of the reading of all of Luke's passion account. Even those who saw Mel Gibson's *The Passion of the Christ* may not remember it or its significance.

I explore this passage on three levels. It occurs in the final section of Luke's Gospel: Jesus' Passion, Death, and Resurrection, and is part of Luke's portrayal of Jesus as an innocent martyr, a righteous person who, although innocent, suffers. See the refrain of innocence in Luke 23:4 (Pilate), 23:14-15 (Pilate and Herod), 23:22 (Pilate), 23:41 (Good Thief), and 23:47 (centurion).

Although the actual word "sinner" is not found in 23:39-43, it is clear from the words of the Good Thief that he considers himself a sinner: "And indeed, we have been condemned justly, for the sentence we received corresponds to our crimes, but this man has done nothing criminal" (23:41). Furthermore, the Good Thief not only acknowledges his sins, but also asks that Jesus remember him in his kingly power. St. Gregory the Great wrote well of the Good Thief: "A great grace shines forth in this thief. Although punishment holds captive his every member except his heart and tongue, he offers what he is free to give. He believes with his heart and confesses with his tongue." In his commentary, St. Ambrose remarks: "What a most exquisite example of a desirable conversion: that forgiveness is so quickly lavished on the thief and the grace he receives far exceeds his plea. For the Lord God always gives more than is asked for."

My final observation focuses on a single word, "Paradise": "Today you will be with me in Paradise." As you can well imagine in a chapter on Jesus, sinners, and food, I am going to maintain that "Paradise" refers to eating of fruit as in the original Garden of Paradise. If you ask me for my evidence, I cite two parallel passages. The first is from a very familiar book, Revelation. Revelation 2:7 reads: "To the victor I will give the right to eat of the tree of life that is in the Paradise of God." To someone who is victorious as the Good Thief will be, through the Lord's intervention, there will be eating of the tree of life in God's Paradise. A Jewish book that flourished at Luke's time bears the name of the *Testaments of the Twelve Patriarchs*. On their deathbeds these patriarchs gave to their children commands and encouragement. *Testament of Levi* 18:10-11 promises that at the end: "He (the priest) will open the gates of Paradise and will remove the sword that has threatened since Adam, and he will grant to the saints to eat of the tree of life."

Am I stretching things too far to find a reference to Jesus eating food with sinners such as the Good Thief in Paradise? If Luke didn't make so much of the imagery of food, then I might be crazed to find a food reference in the word Paradise. But as the scholars say: In descriptions of the final days, what happened in the primitive days is repeated. So if there was eating in Paradise in the beginning of time, so there will be eating in Paradise at the end of time.

Conclusion

In Luke's Gospel, Jesus, sinners, and food go together. As Jesus insists, he has come to call sinners, to save what was lost. He does so over tables of food. Could Luke make the Christian doctrine of the Incarnation more palpable? Could Luke champion an inclusive table more vociferously? In the next chapter I present Jesus at table with those who do not call themselves "sinners." Maybe those righteous who invite Jesus to recline at table with them also need conversion.

Suggested Questions for Reflection

1. Perhaps you've seen the bumper sticker "In case of the rapture this vehicle will be unmanned." This nonbiblical teaching tells us that at the end, the Lord Jesus raptures the saints to be with him and leaves sinners behind. Is this the Lord Jesus that Luke, artist and theologian, paints?

2. When a Franciscan priest recently became a bishop, his friends were jousting that the motto on his coat of arms should be "Fax'm and phon'm"—a take off on *Pax et bonum* (Peace and all good). Do you think that a good motto for a bishop would be "friend of toll collectors and sinners"? Would such a motto be too scandalous, especially if joined with "glutton and drunkard"?

Suggestions for Further Reading

Resseguie, James L. *Spiritual Landscape: Images of the Spiritual Life in the Gospel of Luke*. Peabody, MA: Hendrickson, 2003, 69–87 (Chapter 4: Meals: Spirituality of Hospitality).

Chapter 4

Jesus as Guest, Host, and Teacher at Meals

In this chapter I will explore five passages: Luke 7:36-50, 9:10-17, 11:37-54, 14:1-14, and 24:11-35. I have grouped these passages around the categories of Jesus as guest, as host, and as teacher at meals. In three of these selections, Jesus is reclining at table as a guest in a Pharisee's house: 7:36-50, 11:37-54, and 14:1-14. He seizes the opportunity to teach a lesson to his hosts. In Luke 9:10-17, Jesus is the host who feeds 5,000 people in the desert. He doesn't care whether the 5,000 are Pharisees or not, clean or unclean, rich or poor. They all eat from the abundant table he supplies. In Luke 24:11-35 Jesus is the stranger who is befriended by two of his disciples who have abandoned his way. After Jesus has taught them the meaning of the Scriptures, the disciples invite him to their table where Jesus becomes the host and breaks the bread.

In the last chapter we explored passages in which Luke put Jesus, sinners, and food together. Sinners, you recall, were those who missed the mark by not obeying the Law. May there be some irony in Jesus' table fellowship with Pharisees, who since 6:11 have been hostile to Jesus? From Luke's perspective, are the righteous Pharisees actually self-righteous and therefore sinners, who need the ministrations of Jesus, the physician? At Easter time it is very easy to sentimentalize the story of the two disciples on the way to Emmaus and miss the point that these two disciples are sinners because they have abandoned God's way in Jesus and are running away from God's revelations in Jerusalem. In sum, in these passages Luke presents Jesus with a table napkin on his lap, thrusting himself into the lives of people to lead them away from sin and to God.

Detective Oliver Weeks is a character in Ed McBain's 87th precinct mysteries. His nickname is "Fat Ollie." There's hardly a scene in which Fat Ollie appears that he's not eating. Although bright and even witty, Fat Ollie seems to exist in McBain's books to eat enormous quantities of food, and often. It is repulsive to this reader, at least, to imagine eating the three jumbo pizzas Fat Ollie eats as a snack. Fat Ollie seems to be the character through which McBain criticizes American eating habits. In his own way Luke also uses food to develop his story, for he is heir to a literary tradition that utilized meal or symposium scenes to promote plot and message. For example, Apuleius utilizes meal scenes in his *Metamorphoses* or *The Golden Ass* to further his plot. Toward the end of the story, Lucius, whom Fate had turned into an ass, is close to being changed back into a man. His owner is described: "This is the man who owns as companion and dinner guest an ass who wrestles, an ass who dances, an ass who understands men's language and can say what he wants by nods" (X.17). Meal scenes also convey Apuleius's message, for it is not happenstance that Lucius overcomes Fate and is changed back into a man by eating the roses held in the hand of a priest of the goddess Isis (XI.11-13). In brief, Luke has embraced the storytelling skills of his time and has used them to enhance what tradition said about Jesus at meals.

The Woman Who Is a Sinner Extends Hospitality to Jesus—Luke 7:36-50

I remind my readers that I have a sign that reads: "No whining here!" Sure, this passage is a warmed-up leftover from last chapter, but as they say in the food trade, it has been enhanced. Enjoy.

As we learned last chapter, the woman of this story is neither Mary Magdalene nor a prostitute. As we learned in chapter 2, this story takes place at a symposium meal, at which Jesus is reclining. Further and perhaps most important is the fact that the woman bursts upon the scene at the home of a Pharisee. Luke is employing what the tradition of symposium meals called "the extraordinary event" that stops the action and calls attention to itself. I give a quick example. In his satire about philosophers at a wedding symposium, Lucian of Samosata tells of such an event when Hetoemocles the Stoic sent his servant to a wedding banquet to read a message. In part Hetoemocles's message read: "I have reason to be angry, because you, to whom I have so long ministered indefatigably, did not think fit to number me among your friends. No, I alone do not count with you, and that too though I live next door. I am indignant, therefore, and more on your account than on my own, because you have shown yourself so thankless" (no. 22 of *The Carousal or the Lapiths* in Loeb Classical Library). Hetoemocles, who, as a Stoic, should be able to control his emotions in a "stoic" manner, cannot forgive the host for not inviting him, and you can well imagine the flap this self-serving message created. It was "the extraordinary event" that stopped the action. Whereas Lucian continues his tale of what happened at the wedding symposium, Luke does not. The sinful woman has not only stopped the action, but has also stolen the show. We must await another meal of Jesus with a Pharisee to see how they get along at meals. Luke will not disappoint us, as he presents another one in his travel narrative of Jesus going up to Jerusalem (Luke 11:37–54).

Luke tells this story with consummate skill as he first describes the actions of the woman, then Jesus' parable, and finally Simon the Pharisee's lack of hospitality. Note these sharply phrased contrasts:

> Then Jesus turned to the woman and said to Simon, "Do you see this woman? When I entered your house, you did not give me water for my feet, but she has bathed them with her tears and wiped them with her hair. You did not give me a kiss, but she has not ceased kissing my feet since the time I entered. You

did not anoint my head with oil, but she anointed my feet with ointment" (7:44-46).

If Simon the Pharisee regarded Jesus as a prophet, he might well have shown him these tokens of hospitality.

But this story is not just about a Pharisee's lack of hospitality to Jesus, but it is also about his lack of love. Since Simon has judged himself to have been forgiven a slight debt, he manifests less love to the person who has forgiven him. On the other hand, the sinful woman has acknowledged the great debt her sin has incurred, has received forgiveness, and shows her love through her generous actions.

What does Luke say about Jesus through the account of this symposium meal? Since it comes on the heels of Luke's portrayal of Jesus as "friend of toll collectors and sinners" (7:34), it is a parade example of Jesus' friendship of sinners. Jesus does not ward off sinners from touching him (7:39). Jesus is indeed a prophet (7:39), but even more. Jesus' fellow recliners at the symposium realize as much and ask, almost rhetorically: "Who is this who even forgives sins?" (7:49). To the sinful woman of faith Jesus gives peace (7:50). Simon got more than he bargained for when he invited Jesus, for Jesus not only taught him a lesson about hospitality, but also about forgiveness of those sinners whom Simon had put outside the ranks of the righteous.

Jesus Violates Norms of Hospitality and Teaches Almsgiving as a New Law of Purity— Luke 11:37-54

In chapter 2 we saw that readers can identify a theme by frequency and unexpectedness of occurrence. Luke 11:37-54 describes Jesus' second meal with a Pharisee and suggests that Jesus ate with them with some frequency. Luke 11:37-54 also fits the criterion of the unexpected, for its parallel in Matthew 23:23-36 has similar attacks on the Pharisees and scribes, but without Luke's meal setting. Jesus' meal with a Pharisee is the first of two that Luke recounts in his travel narrative (9:51–19:27) wherein he depicts Jesus traveling to Jerusalem and his death and resurrection. During his journey, Jesus teaches his disciples about his way and corrects the conduct of the Pharisees and scribes. This is the first time in Luke's Gospel that Jesus excoriates the Pharisees for their views on ritual purity, and he does so at a meal. When Mark 7:1-23 and Matthew 1:1-20 present Jesus' attacks against the Pharisees and the scribes for their views on ritual purity, there is no meal setting.

"The extraordinary event" in this symposium meal seems to be Jesus' ability to read the Pharisee's amazed face, to see the negative judgment thereon, and then to launch into an blistering attack against the Pharisees and scribes for not observing genuine purity of heart (11:38-39). On one level, Jesus violates the norms of hospitality, since he inveighs against his host. If you want to get on Luke's wavelength, think of those times when a guest in your house has changed TV channels on you or put the thermostat up ten degrees without your knowledge. Is Jesus consistent, for didn't he earlier take Simon to task for Simon's lack of hospitality? On another level, Luke has led us readers through his previous ten chapters to identify positively with Jesus. Luke's readers, at least this one, may well tolerate Jesus' breaking of the norms of hospitality, for Jesus is correcting abuses and teaching his new system of purity to his disciples.

A brief comment on Luke 11:41 will conclude my observations. Jesus teaches that his new system of purity has its center in almsgiving. Each year much is written on Luke's theme of rich and poor. In these writings the common thread is that Luke insists that one's inner love of God and neighbor must be expressed in an external, concrete way by caring for the needy. Recall that wealthy, chief toll collector Zacchaeus, whom the people considered a sinner, gives half of his possessions to the poor as a sign of his commitment to God and of his repentance (19:1-10). If Jesus' teaching in Luke 7:36-50 was about forgiveness of sin, his teaching in this meal with a Pharisee focuses on almsgiving as the central plank of his new way of ritual purity. Luke does not provide his readers with the response, if any, that the Pharisees and the scribes gave to Jesus' new way of being ritually pure. Rather, Luke ends this symposium meal on an ominous note: "When Jesus left, the scribes and Pharisees began to act with hostility toward him and to interrogate him about many things, for they were plotting to catch him at something he might say" (11:53-54). It should not surprise us that the Pharisees set a trap for Jesus at a meal (14:1-24).

Upping the Ante as a Leader of the Pharisees Takes on Jesus—Luke 14:1-14

Just a moment ago I discussed Jesus' second meal with a Pharisee. Within a very short time Jesus is back at it, eating with the Pharisees who are watching him carefully. The invitation for this third meal with the Pharisees comes from headquarters, from one of the rulers of the Pharisees. If lower-ranking Pharisees can't handle Jesus, one of the leaders will surely take care of him.

From the two previous scenes of Jesus eating with Pharisees, we have come to expect that Jesus will be teaching them. After all, that is fitting behavior at a symposium meal that generally consists of food followed by drinking and conversation or teaching. But before we get to Jesus' teaching, "the extraordinary event" of this banquet scene appears, almost out of nowhere. A man with dropsy is at the meal (14:2). I grant that Jesus cures this man on a Sabbath, justifies his action, and silences the Pharisees and scholars of the Law (14:3-6). Further, I grant that the man with dropsy anticipates "the poor, the crippled, the lame, the blind" of whom Jesus speaks in 14:13 and 14:21. Yet I wonder why Luke mentions a man with this particular illness. Willi Braun and St. Bonaventure have opened my eyes to spot the significance of this specific disease.

Dropsy is an illness whereby a person is bloated with water and has an unquenchable thirst for more water. The more the sick person drinks, the worse he gets. For years I thought of this illness in a theoretical way. One day, after preaching about this passage, a confrere said that he had known a person with dropsy. Bill Smith, bloated almost beyond recognition, would board the school bus with a gallon of water in each hand and would drink and drink, never satisfying his thirst. He finally drank himself to death, overwhelming his system with water. Among the people of Luke's time, a person with dropsy was a symbol of the avaricious person, for the greedy individual had abundant wealth but always thirsted for more. One source reads: "Diogenes compared money-lovers to people with dropsy: as people with dropsy, though filled with fluid crave drink, so money-lovers, though loaded with money, crave more of it, yet both to their demise. For their desires increase the more they acquire the objects of their craving." In my viewpoint Luke may be pointing ahead to the problem the well-to-do will have with Jesus' teaching about inviting the unfortunate to their banquets. They will need to be cured of their particular form of dropsy so they can be generous to the needy.

Jesus' first teaching to his fellow recliners at the symposium deals with a common enough motif in the symposium literature: squabbling over the choice places. When reclining was governed by strict protocol, it was an honor to be assigned a significant place. People who thought they should have been placed higher would grumble and grouse. Plutarch gives this advice to a person who was grieved that he had been assigned an ignominious place: Be thoroughly agreeable to those placed with you and try to discover in them something that may initiate and nourish a friendship (*Dinner of the Seven Wise Men* no. 149B). Like Plutarch, Jesus gives wise counsel to his fellow guests, but puts a theological spin on his wisdom that is not just for banquets, but for life: "For everyone who exalts himself will be humbled, but the one who humbles himself will be exalted" (14:11).

Jesus is not finished with his teaching, for he next advises his host. In technical terms, Jesus is advocating generalized reciprocity, that is, generosity toward the unfortunate who cannot reciprocate. Family and friends have the wherewithal to engage in horizontal reciprocity, and wealthy neighbors are patrons and engage in vertical reciprocity. But "the poor, the crippled, the lame, and the blind" are unable to engage in any type of reciprocity. Jesus' teaching here is of a piece with the instruction he gave in his Sermon on the Plain: "If you lend money to those from whom you expect repayment, what credit is that to you? Even sinners lend to sinners, and get back the same amount. But rather, love your enemies and do good to them, and lend expecting nothing back; then your reward will be great. . . ." (6:34-35).

In his first meal with Pharisees, Jesus taught forgiveness. In his second, his instruction focused on almsgiving as the true cleansing device. Now here in his third meal with a Pharisee his instruction concerns a person's humble relationship to God and his generous concern for the outcasts. Through his narration of Jesus' meals with Pharisees, Luke makes clear that Jesus is not an ordinary Jewish teacher, for he is teaching the teachers in Israel and contrasting his way with theirs. Jesus will continue to teach at meals, especially at his last earthly meal and in the course of his association with the two disciples on the way to Emmaus. To that story we now turn.

Jesus Is Teacher, Guest, and Host at the Breaking of Bread—Luke 24:13-35

As is my wont, I make some introductory remarks. Religious art can be a legitimate and powerfully persuasive interpreter of Sacred Scripture. Think of how many people are influenced in their theology and piety by Leonardo da Vinci's painting of the *Last Supper*, despite its inadequacies. I must admit that I was captivated by the mural that covers an entire wall of a refectory in a religious community and portrays Cleopas and his wife conversing with the risen Lord Jesus on the road. Further, I plead with my readers to take this meal as one of a sequence of meals in Luke's Gospel. That is, please read it in context. While the breaking of bread or Eucharist is an important element in this story, it is not the whole story. Keep your eyes open to appreciate the other elements that Luke presents in this hauntingly beautiful story.

The motif of journey steps briskly through this narrative. For example, the two disciples were going to a village; Jesus draws near and journeys with them; the disciples' hearts burned as Jesus talked to them on the road; the disciples journey back to Jerusalem where they tell the others what had taken place on the road. The disciples' journey is one from abandonment of the way of Jesus to forgiveness and renewed faith. Their rerouting on their journey takes place because of the stranger's teaching and his breaking of the bread.

There is much teaching in this passage. It is ironic that in 24:19-24 the two disciples recite the Christian creed to Jesus who is the object of the creed. Indeed, he is the prophet mighty in deed and word before God and all the people (Acts 2:22-24; 10:38). They are narrating to Jesus the fulfillment of the prophecies he made in Luke 9:22, 13:32-33, and 18:31-33. Truly it is the third day, the day of reversal and resurrection. The faithful women have proclaimed the Easter kerygma. Further teaching occurs in 24:25-27 when the unrecognized risen Lord Jesus explains the Scriptures to his disciples. It is only with Jesus' breaking of the bread that the two disciples see the truth of the creed they had been reciting to Jesus and acknowledge how he had seared their hearts by his interpretation of the Scriptures. We are not stretching the truth if we connect creed and Scripture interpretation with this meal at which Jesus and the two disciples recline. Teaching at a meal is part and parcel of what happens at meals in Luke. Why should this account be different?

St. Bonaventure was a forerunner of those interpreters who maintain that the disciples' hearts would still be cold and that they would have broken bread by themselves if they had not shown hospitality to a stranger. They welcome the stranger to travel and converse with them and almost force him to stay and eat with them. Hospitality shown prepares for understanding the Scriptures and appreciating the breaking of bread.

Jesus, invited by his two disciples to stay with them as their guest, becomes their host. As he had done in the multiplication of loaves, Jesus "took bread, said the blessing, broke it, and gave it to them" (24:30). The earlier passage of Luke 9:16 reads: "Then taking the five loaves and the two fish, and looking up to heaven, Jesus said the blessing over them, broke them, and gave them to the disciples to set before the crowd." While the Eucharist seems to be in the background, there is no wine and no words of institution over the bread. The point of the story at this juncture is that Jesus, although killed, is alive and continues to share life. Some years ago I said it this way:

> Disciples who entertain the stranger have their eyes opened, and they recognize Jesus because he shares food with them. Graced with the sight of faith, the disciples now see that God's kingly conquest of sin and death . . . comes from opening oneself to the unwanted and unexpected dimensions of Christian discipleship and by extending welcoming hands to strangers. They see how the scriptural promises that God's hungry creation will be fed beyond death at the messianic banquet have come true in the risen Jesus, the invited guest, now turned host, whose wounded hands distribute the bread of life to them.

In conclusion, Matthew 28:1-20 and Mark 16:1-8 do not provide narratives of meals that the risen Lord Jesus had with his disciples. John 21:1-14 comes the closest to Luke 24:13-35, as both evangelists use the symbol of food to describe the risen Lord Jesus' power to provide the food of life to his disciples. But Luke tops John, for he repeats his motif of hospitality, especially to the stranger, and continues his motif of Jesus who teaches at meals.

Jesus, God's Messiah, Welcomes All and Sundry to His Table—Luke 9:10-17

This is the last feeding story in Luke's account of Jesus' Galilean ministry. Earlier, Jesus had reclined at the tables of Levi, a toll collector, and of Simon, a Pharisee. He had been ridiculed as "a glutton and a drunkard and the friend of toll collectors and sinners." Now he is going to host 5,000 people to a meal. The rationalist interpretation of this miracle is very popular today, as it maintains that Jesus' generosity in sharing his five loaves and two fish shamed the 5,000 to share the food they had secreted in the folds of their garments. While this interpretation may promote social justice, it has little basis in the text and diminishes Luke's presentation of Jesus as the provider of the food of life.

As we have seen, context is very important in the interpretation of a passage in Scripture. In Luke 9:7-9 Herod Antipas raises the question about Jesus' identity: Jesus is not John raised from the dead, nor Elijah, nor one of the ancient prophets. After this story in Luke 9:18-21, Jesus asks his disciples what the crowds, who had enjoyed the multiplication of loaves and fish, say about him. Their response is very similar to that of Herod: John the Baptist, Elijah, one of the ancient prophets. Peter, however, gives the correct response: Jesus is God's Messiah (9:20). Thus, Luke is the only one of the four evangelists, who all narrate this incident, to use it to create a literary sandwich. The two pieces of bread are the questions about Jesus' identity. The meat of the sandwich is Jesus' feeding of the 5,000, a miracle that in its turn has contributed to Peter's confession of faith.

If we look very carefully at Luke's account and try to block out what the other three evangelists say, we will notice that for Luke this is not a miracle of compassion for those faint with hunger. Nowhere in Luke 9:10-17 does it say that the 5,000 were starving. Jesus, who welcomes the crowds, becomes the host and reveals who he is as the giver of the food of life. Perhaps God's gift of manna in the desert hovers in the background, as Jesus does what God did for God's people in the desert (see Exodus 16).

A legitimate translation of Luke 9:14 is the one found in the 1963 Confraternity edition: "Make them recline in dining groups of fifties." The more modern NAB reads: "Have them sit down in groups of [about] fifty." As we have seen, Luke is very much concerned with "reclining" and uses a variety of verbs to convey this festive posture. The Greek word *(klisia)* behind "dining group" is rare and occurs in contexts of a king hosting an array of guests who fix their attention, not on one another, but on the king. Archaeological data also suggest that dining facilities were erected in such a way that the diners' attention was on the host, not on one's fellow diner. If you ask about the huge number of 5,000 guests, I remark that there is evidence of a royal banquet to which 69,574 guests were invited. What I am suggesting, as I summarize much data, is that in his account of Jesus' multiplication of loaves, Luke may be drawing his readers' attention to Jesus as the benefactor of the dining groups. The eyes of the dining groups are on the Lord Jesus, who provides the food of the poor (bread and dried fish) for God's hungry people in the desert.

As we have seen in the last chapter and so far in this chapter, the Pharisees were very much concerned with ritual purity, paying tithes on food, sitting with the proper people, and seeking out positions at a symposium that befit their honorable dignity. Jesus goes against the Pharisees' taboos as he has people recline in dining groups of fifty. Jesus shows no concern with regulations of washing before eating and with questions of who eats with whom and what is eaten. This miracle is a glowing example of Jesus' inclusive table, to which he invites sinners and the unclean.

Luke's description of Jesus blessing, breaking, and giving the food (9:16) prepares for Luke 22:16-20 and 24:30. Jesus gives the bread of life to the world and also to his community of believers in the Eucharist.

Conclusion

In this chapter I have grouped five Lukan meal scenes around the title of Jesus as Guest, Host, and Teacher at Meals. To me it is not surprising that Jesus, who had nowhere to lay his head (9:58), would accept dinner invitations. To me it is not surprising that Jesus would teach at meals, for, after all, he was a teacher. What is surprising is that Jesus would host a meal, and what is perhaps even more surprising is that Jesus would dine with people who were his enemies. St. Bonaventure's commentary on Luke 14:1 merits quotation:

> In this action Christ's wonderful kindness is manifest. It is *great* in that he was associating with mortal human beings, although he was God. . . . Indeed, it was *greater* in that he was associating with his persecutors. . . . But his kindness is *greatest*, because his association took the form of intimate sharing of food, so that Revelation 3:20 may be fulfilled: "I stand at the door and knock. If anyone . . . opens the door for me, I will come in to him and will sup with him, and he with me." So through the fact that he entered a strange house, Christ's *humility* is commended. Through the fact that he entered a Pharisee's house, *love*. Through the fact that he ate a stranger's food, *the poverty of Christ himself*. And in these is shown *the highest kindness*, by which *the most high* wanted to be humbled for us, *the most just* to associate with the impious, *the most rich* to become poor among men and women. Wherefore, 2 Corinthians 8:9 says: "You know the graciousness of our Lord Jesus Christ, that, although he was rich, he became poor for our sakes, so that by his poverty we might become rich."

Suggested Questions for Reflection

1. Is there more to Jesus' three meals with Pharisees than his teaching about forgiveness of sins, almsgiving as the means to ritual purity, and care of the outcasts of society? What is that "more"?

2. The famous Italian painter Caravaggio has a magnificent rendition of Jesus' breaking bread with the disciples of Emmaus. Check it out on the Web. The entire focus of the scene is on Jesus, who is sitting, and whose right hand is extended over bread and other foods. There are three male disciples around Jesus. Does this artistic representation of Emmaus tell the whole truth?

3. The New Testament translation of the American Bible Society has an artist's sketch of the 5,000 eating Jesus' gift of bread and fish. How would you sketch the scene, especially in the light of what I have presented in this chapter? If you're as artistic as I am, you'll probably want to use stick women and men.

Suggestions for Further Reading

Bartchy, S. Scott. "The Historical Jesus and Honor Reversal at Table," in Wolfgang Stegemann, and others, eds., *The Social Setting of Jesus and the Gospels*. Minneapolis: Fortress, 2002, 175–83.

Braun, Willi. *Feasting and social rhetoric in Luke 14.* Society of New Testament Studies Monograph Series 85; Cambridge: Cambridge University Press, 1995.

Karris, Robert J. "Food in the Gospel of Luke," *The Bible Today* 38 (6) (November 2000) 357–61.

———. "Luke 24:13-35," *Interpretation* 41 (1987) 57–61.

Wilson, C. K. "Superabundant Table Fellowship in the Kingdom: The Feeding of the Five Thousand and the Meal Motif in Luke," *Expository Times* 114 (7) (April 2003) 224–30.

Chapter 5

Jesus' Petition for Food and Food Imagery in Luke's Parables

We come to yet another dimension of the theme of food in Luke's Gospel. First I consider the petition for food in the Lord's Prayer. This petition connects beautifully and powerfully with the motif of the last chapter, for we all need food and we all eat together at the Lord's table of life and redemption. Within the compass of this book, it is impossible to consider in detail all of Jesus' parables, even those that contain food imagery. In the second part of this chapter I explore the food imagery in Luke's parables to crack open a window onto their meaning and to tease us into digging afresh into some of Luke's parables. In this venture I follow the famous British New Testament scholar C. H. Dodd who offered this definition of a parable: "At its simplest the parable is a metaphor or simile drawn from nature or common life, arresting the hearer by its vividness or strangeness, and leaving the mind in sufficient doubt about its precise application to tease it into active thought" (*Parables*, 5).

Jesus' Petition for Our Daily Bread—Luke 11:3

Luke 11:3 reads: "Give us each day our daily bread." Behind this prayer is the humble acknowledgment that we human beings depend upon God for life and our daily sustenance. Since bread is such a polyvalent symbol, I do not read something into the text when I suggest that petitioners are also asking for food for the life of their spirit and even for the food of Jesus' gift of the Eucharist.

I also call my readers' attention to the repetition in this petition: twice some form of "we" occurs: "us" and "our." In the context of our study so far, this "we" has special significance. We are praying the prayer of Jesus who ate with sinners, toll collectors, and those hostile to him. These are the types of people included in our petition for "our" daily bread. If we want to recognize our total dependence upon the human community for life, we might look at this petition from yet another angle. I love to cook and have pawed through my recipes for the simplest one. It is for beer bread and calls for three cups of self-rising flour, one and a half tablespoons of sugar, and one 12-oz. can of beer at room temperature. After mixing these ingredients together and putting them in a lightly greased pan, you bake them at 350 degrees for one hour. During the last ten minutes the loaf may be brushed with margarine for a golden brown color. Even though this recipe is so simple, I cannot accomplish it by myself. I don't grow self-rising flour or sugar cane in my background. Cans of beer don't grow on the trees in my front lawn. I didn't manufacture the stove either. It is "we" together who have to bake this simple loaf of bread. In a Gospel that talks so much about the dangers of greed (e.g., 12:15) and the need for almsgiving (e.g., 11:41) the "we" also includes those who are less fortunate than we who pray this prayer.

Lukan Parables in Which the Imagery of Food Occurs

There are twenty-three parables in Luke's Gospel, and food occurs in fifteen of them. In my treatment of these fifteen parables I offer a distinction between an incidental, less incidental, and substantial occurrence of food. I arrive at a decision to put a particular parable in a certain category based on the extent to which the food imagery contributes to the meaning of the parable: Does it merely offer a helping hand in Luke's literary kitchen or is it the chef? Since parables have multiple levels of meaning, my decisions may have the result of escorting some meaning out of the kitchen. While I welcome dissent, discussion, and demurring, someone has to help us sort out Luke's food imagery in fifteen of his parables. I will be the sorter and will provide a brief justification for the decision I have made on all fifteen parables. I judge the food imagery to be incidental in the following parables: Luke 8:4-15, 10:30-37, 11:5-8, 12:40-48, 13:6-9, 16:1-8, 17:7-10, 18:9-14, and 20:9-14. It is less incidental in: Luke 12:13-21 and 15:11-32. It is substantial in the parables of Luke 12:35-40, 13:18-21, 14:7-11, 14:15-24, 15:4-7, and 16:19-31.

Lukan Parables in Which the Image of Food Is Incidental

At the beginning of this section, I caution my readers. Although I may judge Luke's food imagery in a particular parable to be incidental, I do not mean that its food imagery is insignificant and to be tossed into the garbage pail. Even actors with a tiny part in a play contribute to its overall success.

Luke 8:4-15 has four dimensions, depending upon whether the interpreter stresses the seed, the sower, the types of soil, or the harvest. While seed will eventually lead to food on the table, this parable and its interpretation move away from the table into what's in a person's heart and the power of the Word to provide an astonishing large harvest. Put another way, the food dimension in this parable makes an incidental contribution to its successful telling.

The parable of the Good Samaritan (10:30-37) is so familiar in its general lines that we often rush past some of its details. One such incidental detail is that the Samaritan poured olive oil and wine onto the beaten man's wounds and bandaged them (10:34). While both olive oil and wine have nutritive and medicinal purposes, their occurrence in this parable is not substantial. That is, the point of the story would be the same whether the Samaritan showed his compassion by simply bandaging the wounds to arrest the man's bleeding.

The parable of Luke 11:5-8 is not really about one friend loaning another friend three loaves of bread (11:5), but about the shameless persistence of the petitioner at a most inconvenient time of the day. Thus, the need for "three loaves of bread," while the occasion for the friend's pounding on the door at midnight is incidental in this parable.

Luke 12:41-48 provides an interpretation of the parable of 12:35-40. In this interpretation the unfaithful steward is the one who beats the menservants and maidservants. He eats, drinks, and gets drunk from the provisions he is supposed to oversee (12:45). His eating and drinking to excess are examples of behavior that the master will punish severely. Like the action of beating one's fellow servants, they are incidental to the substance of the explanation, namely, the servant's fidelity. Of a piece with Luke 12:35-48 is Luke 17:7-10. This parable notes that the servant's waiting on his master while he eats and drinks is like plowing or tending sheep. It is part of the servant's job and does not merit a claim for extra pay. That is, the food imagery buttresses one example of the servant's obligations to his master and is not the substance of the account.

The parable of the barren fig tree (Luke 13:6-9) has echoes with Old Testament texts such as Micah 7:1 where the prophet bemoans the fact that Israel has not been productive: "Alas! I am as when the fruit is gathered, as when the vines have been gleaned. There is no cluster of grapes to eat, no early fig that I crave." This echo between the Testaments and the one-year reprieve the fig tree gets suggest that repentance, not food, is the gist of this parable. Figs, so succulent to eat, are incidental to this parable.

Luke 16:1-8 says that the steward reduces the promissory note for "850 gallons of olive oil" by half and the one for "1,100 bushels of wheat" by 20 percent. In my way of thinking, "finished stones for building" or "cords of wood" might easily be substituted for olive oil and wheat. That is, the mention of foodstuffs is incidental to the point of the parable: the shrewdness of the "dishonest" manager.

The parable of the Pharisee and the toll collector in Luke 18:9-14 provides another example of an incidental use of the theme of food. That the Pharisee fasts twice a week (18:12) helps make the point that the Pharisee goes beyond the requirements of the Law. The Pharisee might well have mentioned that he gives alms.

Luke 20:9-19 tells of a vineyard and the tenants' failure to share its fruits with the owner. It also tells of the tenants' hostile behavior toward the owner's servants and son. Isaiah 5:1-7 speaks about God's planting a vineyard, which is Israel. Although more muted than in Mark 12:1-12 and Matthew 21:33-46, echoes of Isaiah 5:1-7 still come across loud and clear in Luke 20:9-19. That the tenants did not send the owner grapes to eat and wine to drink seems incidental to the parable's message. Their evil treatment of the owner's servants and son and the owner's response to their actions convey the substance of the parable.

Lukan Parables in Which the Food Imagery Is Less Incidental

Luke 12:13-21 contains the parable of what a rich man does with his abundant harvest. Viewed in this light, this parable certainly deals with foodstuffs. But when viewed within the context in which Luke has set this parable, this parable aids Jesus' teaching against greed. See especially Luke 12:15, the verse that introduces the parable: "Then Jesus said to the crowd, 'Take care to guard against all greed, for though one may be rich, one's life does not consist of possessions.'" In a recent class on this parable, one participant aptly titled this parable: "Big barn, but small heart." In any case, I judge that the food imagery of this parable, while not substantial, is more than incidental.

There is an abundant table of food imagery in the parable of the Prodigal Son (15:11-32). Luke 15:14, 17, dwell on famine and starvation. Luke 15:15-16 mention pigs, a choice food of non-Jews. "The fattened calf" occurs no less than three times

(15:23, 27, 30). The elder son notes in resentment that his father had never even given him a young goat for a party with his friends (15:29). While the aromas of these meats waft from the verses of this parable and capture our attention, they do not pertain to the substance of the parable which is about the father's forgiveness of the wastrel, runaway younger son and the stubborn resentment of the elder son. Since the fattened calf occurs thrice and would be enough luscious meat for one hundred fifty people from family and village, I judge the food imagery of this parable to be less than incidental.

Lukan Parables in Which Food Imagery Is Substantial

The parable in Luke 12:35-40 talks about the reward that the master gives to vigilant servants: "He will gird himself, have them recline at table, and proceed to wait on them" (12:37). Although no food is explicitly mentioned, food is surely implied in the words "reclining at table" and "wait on them." Why the food imagery? Couldn't the master have just given the vigilant servant a bonus or his freedom? Within the entire framework of Luke's Gospel that deals so much with food, I would judge this type of reward to be of the substance of the parable.

It does not seem happenstance that Luke concludes the first section of Jesus' journey to Jerusalem with two short parables about the kingdom of God that Jesus has been revealing in his teaching and healing ministry (13:18-21). For example, in 13:10-17 Luke narrates how Jesus has freed a daughter of Abraham who had been in bondage for eighteen years. The first parable reads: "Therefore, what is the kingdom of God like? To what can I compare it? It is like a mustard seed that a person took and planted in his garden. When it was fully grown, it became a tree and the birds of the sky dwelt in its branches." If we compare Luke's version to those of Mark 4:3-32 and Matthew 13:31-32, we notice a number of things. First, Luke does not call the mustard seed "the smallest of all seeds." Second, whereas Mark 4:37 says that the mustard seed is sown upon the ground and Matthew 13:31 that it is sown in the person's field, Luke alone states that it is sown "in his garden." Most Gospel commentators, even those who comment on Luke's Gospel, make the point of Jesus' parable the contrast between smallness of the mustard seed and the greatness of the bunch that results. You see, a mustard seed has a diameter a tad longer than one millimeter, and its takes some 750 mustard seeds to weigh one gram (= .035 oz.). When fully grown, though, it is taller than Shaquille O'Neal.

Luke's point seems to be different, as he alone has the farmer sow the mustard seed in his garden. In his *Natural History* 19.170-171, Pliny the Elder adds another dimension for our interpretation of the parable:

> . . . and mustard, which with its pungent taste and fiery effect is extremely beneficial for the health. It grows entirely wild, though it is improved by being transplanted: but on the other hand when it has once been sown it is scarcely possible to get the place free of it, as the seed when it falls germinates at once. It is also used to make a relish, by being boiled down in saucepans till its sharp flavour ceases to be noticeable; also its leaves are boiled, like those of all other vegetables (Loeb Classical Library).

While mustard may well supply tasty greens and a tangy condiment, it can forcefully take over a garden if the farmer lets it. Further, the birds that it attracts in its branches do no favors to the rest of the garden. I offer this interpretation of Luke 13:18-19: If you let the kingdom of God enter your heart, it will take over as the mustard plant does, but will supply you with nourishment and add spice to your life.

Luke's second short parable in Luke 13:20-21 is: "To what shall I compare the kingdom of God? It is like yeast that a woman took and hid in forty pounds of wheat flour until the whole batch of dough was leavened" (author's translation). This same parable occurs verbatim in Matthew 13:33. Let me explore more at length the ingredients of this parable. Yeast is a corrupting substance, yet it functions positively in this parable.

Normally translations talk about "three measures of flour." I have taken the liberty to convert "three measures of flour" into more understandable modern terms. I justify my interpretation by quoting the parable expert Arland J. Hultgren:

> The amount in question, therefore, is roughly 4.5 pecks, 1.125 bushels, or 144 cups. That would weigh about 40 pounds (a 5-pound bag of flour yields about 18 cups). Modern recipes typically call for 3.5 cups of flour to make a good-sized loaf of bread. Using that as a standard, the amount of flour in question would easily make 40 generous-sized loaves of bread—60 or even 80 small ones (*The Parables of Jesus: A Commentary*. Grand Rapids: Eerdmans, 2000, 407).

It would seem that the woman would need a bathtub in which to prepare her dough. Why is she preparing so much bread? Since the custom in Roman Palestine was to bake bread once a week for the entire family or even immediate neighborhood, that would help explain the large number of loaves baked. But this custom doesn't explain why the woman, presumed to be of modest means, is using the best and most expensive wheat flour rather than the more common and cheap barley flour (see chapter 1). There's another mystery in the text. The Greek (*ekrypsen*) is very clear: The woman *hid* the yeast. The NAB and NRSV seem to follow standard baking procedures by offering the translation "she mixed in" for *ekrypsen*. Yet the very point of the parable is that the woman does not mix the yeast with the forty pounds of flour! There are two truly odd things about this parable: the woman does not knead the yeast into the flour, and she does not add any liquid to it. Any bread recipe that I know of calls for liquid to be added to the flour, be it warm water, apricot juice, or even alcohol. The parable emphasizes the power of the yeast to turn a massive amount of dry, expensive flour into most tasty and satisfying nourishment for many people with little human agency involved. How long will it take the yeast to work? Jesus doesn't give a time frame. He is using food imagery to talk about the power of God's rule.

In our last chapter we looked at the parable of Luke 14:7-14 that Jesus delivers during the course of a meal with the Pharisees. It goes without saying that food imagery is of the very substance of this parable that addresses the proper way of seeking places at a symposium meal.

The food imagery of the great banquet in the parable of Luke 14:15-24 is also substantial. Without it there is no parable. I make two further comments on this parable. First, Matthew 22:1-14 provides a parallel to Luke 14:15-24, but does not have Luke 14:18-19, the section that contains the excuses of those invited. Two of the people who excuse themselves seem to be rich enough to buy a field as an absentee landlord and to purchase five yoke of oxen. Five yoke of oxen are not needed to plow a peasant's small plot of land, but 100 acres, which would be a large track of land in Roman Palestine. Second, Luke 14:21 repeats in just a slightly different order the invitation list from Luke 14:13: "The poor and maimed and blind and lame." In the document that governed its life, the community at Qumran near the Dead Sea listed the following people as those forbidden entry to the messianic banquet: afflicted in flesh, crushed in feet or hands, lame, blind, deaf, dumb, defective eyesight, senility. Many of us senior citizens with our various ailments wouldn't stand a chance of getting a place at that table. I conclude by stating that this parable is of a piece with the rest of Luke's Gospel that presents God as going out in Jesus to society's outcasts at meals. After all, Jesus is the glutton and drunkard, the friend of toll collectors and sinners.

Luke 15:4-7 is the first of three parables about what has been lost: a sheep, a coin, a son. The shepherd goes in pursuit of his lost sheep because its wool and meat are valuable. The economical aspects of warm clothing and lamb chops seem to pertain to the substance of this parable whose main point is the recovery of something significant that was lost.

Luke 16:19-31 makes no sense without the imagery of food. Hear again these references to food. Jesus says: "There was a rich man who . . . dined sumptuously on a daily basis. And lying at his door was a poor man named Lazarus, covered with sores, who would gladly have eaten his fill from the scraps that fell from the rich man's table. Dogs even used to come and lick his sores" (16:19-21). Lazarus is given the place of honor at Abraham's banquet table and rests on Abraham's bosom (16:23). From his torment in the netherworld the rich man acknowledges that he knows Lazarus' name and asks for water (16:24). Clearly the reversal theme that Luke announced in Mary's *Magnificat* shines forth: "The hungry he has filled with good things. The rich he has sent away empty" (1:53). Clearly food imagery is of the substance of this parable.

Conclusion

Every time disciples repeat the prayer that Jesus left them, he challenges them to continue his inclusive table fellowship: Give US today OUR daily bread. As we will see in our next chapter, it is the same challenge that Jesus will repeat after the institution of the Eucharist: "Do this in memory of me" (22:19). "This" does not merely refer to Jesus' words over the bread, but also to the table fellowship he had with all and sundry during his ministry in Galilee and on his journey to Jerusalem.

Since many of us often encounter the Lukan parables in the tidbits offered by the weekly Lectionary, we may have missed the theme of food that runs through some 70 percent of them. Food imagery makes these parables tick and helps them to achieve their goal of teasing us to taste afresh God's rule in our world, our community, and our very hearts.

Suggested Questions for Reflection

1. Read Luke 16:19-31 slowly, concentrating on verses 27-31. What do the rich man's brothers have to do to avoid joining their brother in the torments of the netherworld? What do Moses and the Prophets say that might prompt the brothers to change their lives?

2. How might we invite the blind, lame, maimed, and poor to our tables? Are the people at Qumran the only people who have restricted access to their holy table?

3. How is the kingdom of God like a mustard seed, like leaven in our world, our church, our family, our lives?

4. You have read my sorting out of the food imagery in Luke's parables. If I've done a good job, praise the Lord. If I've botched the job, how would you correct my sorting?

Suggestions for Further Reading

Gillman, John. *Possessions and the Life of Faith: A Reading of Luke–Acts.* Zachaeus Studies: New Testament Series. Collegeville: Liturgical Press, 1991.

Karris, Robert J. *Prayer and the New Testament: Jesus and His Communities at Prayer.* New York: Crossroad, 2000, 19–24, 64–68.

Phillips, Thomas E. "Reading Recent Readings of Issues of Wealth and Poverty in Luke and Acts," *Currents in Biblical Research* 1.2 (2003) 231–69.

Reid, Barbara E. *Parables for Preachers: The Gospel of Luke Year C.* Collegeville: Liturgical Press, 2000.

Resseguie, James L. *Spiritual Landscape: Images of the Spiritual Life in the Gospel of Luke.* Peabody, MA: Hendrickson, 2003, 101–14.

Rohrbaugh, Richard L. "A Dysfunctional Family and Its Neighbours (Luke 15:11b-32)." In V. George Shillington, ed., *Jesus and His Parables: Interpreting the Parables of Jesus Today.* Edinburgh: T & T Clark, 1997, 141–64.

Chapter 6

Trawling for the Theme of Food in the Gospels of John, Mark, and Matthew

When I teach, I try to abide by the proverb: If I give you a fish, you eat for today. If I teach you how to fish, you eat for life. Now that you have mastered the fishing techniques of finding and interpreting the theme of food in Luke, you can readily apply them to the Gospels of Matthew, Mark, and John. By contrasting what these three Gospels say about food with Luke's emphasis on this theme, we may perhaps find that these other Gospels do not elevate food to the level of a theme in their presentation of Jesus and that Luke is unique. To get you started I will briefly trawl with you in the Gospel of John.

The Theme of Food in John's Gospel

The first step in working our way through the twenty-one chapters that comprise John's Gospel is to note the occurrences of food imagery. We are looking for both frequency and the unexpected in these occurrences (see chapter 2). In addition, as we enter the classroom in our search for the theme of food in John, we must check at the door the template of a harmonized version of the Gospels. Let John be John. Put another way, don't read John as Luke, even though that may be the dominant

Gospel in your mind right now. Finally, don't peek at what my investigation of this theme in John has surfaced. Do your own work first. Then you'll be in a position to correct mine.

John 1:26, 31, 33	John baptizes with water.
John 1:19	Jesus is the Lamb of God, who takes away the sin of the world.
John 1:32	John saw the Spirit come down like a dove from the sky.
John 1:36	Behold, the Lamb of God.
John 1:48	Jesus tells Nathanael: I saw you under the fig tree.
John 2:1-12	Jesus turns water into abundant and superb wine.
John 2:13-22	At Passover, Jesus drove from the Temple those selling oxen, sheep, and doves, and has special words for those selling doves.
John 3:5	No one can enter God's kingdom without being born of water and Spirit.
John 3:22-30	Disputes over baptizing with water.
John 4:1	Jesus is baptizing.
John 4:4-26	Jesus' dialogue with the woman of Samaria about water.
John 4:31-38	Jesus' disciples return with food (see 4:8), but Jesus' food is to do the will of the one who sent him. Image of harvest and reapers.
John 5:2	In Jerusalem there is a Sheep Gate.
John 6:1-15	Jesus multiplies the five barley loaves and two fish near the feast of Passover. No mention that the five thousand were famished.
John 6:26-50	Bread of life and drink that quenches thirst (6:35).
John 6:51-59	Unless you eat the flesh of the Son of Man and drink his blood. . . .
John 7:37-39	Jesus says: Let anyone who thirsts come to me. . . .

John 9:7	Jesus tells the man born blind: Go, wash in the Pool of Siloam. . . .
John 9:11	Go to Siloam and wash. . . .
John 9:15	He put clay on my eyes, and I washed, and now I can see.
John 10:1-18	Sheep, sheepfold, shepherd, and wolf.
John 10:26	You are not among my sheep.
John 10:27	My sheep heard my voice. . . .
John 10:40	Where John first baptized.
John 11:55	The Passover of the Jews was near.
John 12:2	Martha, Mary, and Lazarus give a dinner for Jesus.
John 12:14-15	Jesus rides into Jerusalem on an ass.
John 12:24	Grain of wheat must die to give life.
John 13:3	During the supper before the feast of Passover.
John 13:4-17	Jesus washes disciples' feet and explains his action.
John 13:18	But so that the Scripture might be fulfilled, "The one who ate my food has raised his heel against me."
John 13:26-27	Morsel that Jesus dips and offers to Judas.
John 13:38	Cock will not crow before you deny me thrice.
John 15:1-10	Jesus, true vine, disciples as branches that bear fruit.
John 18:11	Shall I not drink the cup that the Father gave me?
John 18:27	Again Peter denied it, and immediately the cock crowed.
John 18:28	They themselves did not enter the praetorium, in order not to be defiled so that they could eat the Passover.
John 18:39	You have a custom that I release one prisoner to you at Passover.
John 19:14	It was preparation day for Passover.
John 19:28	Jesus says: I thirst.

John 19:29	Jesus is offered a sip of common wine.
John 19:34	Blood and water flow from Jesus' wounded side.
John 21:1-14	Risen Jesus provides a catch of 153 huge fish and a meal of bread and fish.
John 21:15-17	Peter is to feed Jesus' sheep.
John 21:20	Beloved Disciple is the one who had reclined upon Jesus' chest during the supper.

Even though I'm quite familiar with the Gospel of John, I was still amazed to see how many references to food imagery occur in it. If you compare John's Gospel with Matthew, Mark, and Luke, you would see that a significant number of passages in John are unique or unexpected. Let me list some of the main ones: Jesus' turns water into wine at Cana in Nazareth (2:1-11); Jesus tells the Samaritan woman about living water (4:4-26); Jesus' food is to do the will of the one who sent him (4:31-38); Jesus gives an interpretation of his multiplication of loaves and is the Bread of Life (6:26-59); Jesus is the Good Shepherd for his sheep (10:1-16); Jesus is the true Vine (15:1-10); on the cross Jesus says: I thirst (19:28). Moreover, there seems to be constant reference to Passover, when the paschal lambs were slain.

The evidence seems cogent to draw the conclusion that food is indeed a theme in John's Gospel. The task for the student, then, is to interpret this extensive and impressive data. In her recent study, Jane S. Webster has provided students with a very helpful analysis of the significance of food imagery in John. Rather than repeat Webster's analysis, I would suggest my own approach to my readers. In our study of Luke's Gospel the main references to drink occurred in the slur that Jesus was a drunkard and at Jesus' final earthly meal with his disciples. In John's Gospel, however, references to drink abound. John's Gospel begins with a reference to Jesus' sign of turning water into wine and ends with Jesus saying "I thirst" and with water flowing from the crucified Jesus' pierced side. Between those two points Jesus reveals himself to the Samaritan woman as living water, discourses about the true drink of the Eucharist, proclaims at the feast of Tabernacles that thirsty folk will find satisfying drink in him, gives sight to the man born blind by having him wash in the Pool of Siloam (which means Sent), and washes his disciples' feet. In all these instances I suggest that we ask the question I proposed during the course of my study of food symbolism in Luke's Gospel: What does this drink imagery say about Jesus? Is John saying that just as human beings cannot live without water, so too they cannot live without the revelation of God's love in Jesus?

I stop here, for I am confident that my readers have gotten the point and are ready to commence fishing on their own in the waters of John's Gospel that are shallow enough for a child to wade in and deep enough for a whale to frolic in.

The Theme of Food in Mark's Gospel

We should not be surprised that some references to food that we met in our study of Luke's Gospel will also turn up in Mark's Gospel, for it is commonly assumed that Mark was one of Luke's sources. Yet this common assumption does not absolve us from studying Mark's Gospel on its own terms. I again plead with my readers to do their own independent listing of the references to food in Mark's Gospel and not look ahead and steal a glance at my listing.

Mark 1:5	John baptizes.
Mark 1:6	John dressed in camel's hair and fed on locusts and wild honey.
Mark 1:8	I baptize with water. He will baptize you with the Holy Spirit.
Mark 1:9	Jesus is baptized.
Mark 1:10	Jesus saw . . . the Spirit descending like a dove.
Mark 1:16	Simon and Andrew are fishermen.
Mark 1:17	Jesus will make them fishers of men and women.

Mark 1:19	Jesus calls two other fishermen, James and John.
Mark 1:31	Simon's mother-in-law waits on them.
Mark 1:44	Jesus commands the cleansed leper to offer what Moses prescribed.
Mark 2:13-17	Jesus at table in Levi's house with many toll collectors and sinners. Scribes and Pharisees question Jesus' disciples about his eating with such people.
Mark 2:18-22	Proper time to fast and the proper container for new wine.
Mark 2:23-28	Disciples eat grain on the Sabbath.
Mark 4:1-20	Parable of the sower and its interpretation.
Mark 4:26-29	Parable of the seed that grows without sower's assistance.
Mark 4:30-32	Parable of mustard seed.
Mark 5:1-20	Two thousand hogs drown in the sea.
Mark 5:43	Jesus commands that the twelve-year-old girl he has resuscitated be given food.
Mark 6:8	The Twelve are to take food for their journey.
Mark 6:13	Apostles anointed with olive oil many who were sick and cured them.
Mark 6:21	Herod's birthday banquet.
Mark 6:26, 28	On a food platter is the head of John the Baptist.
Mark 6:31	Things were so hectic that Jesus and the Twelve had no opportunity to eat.
Mark 6:34-44	Jesus multiplies five loaves and two fish for 5,000. Twelve baskets of fragments are collected.
Mark 7:2-3, 5	Scribes and Pharisees observe that some of Jesus' disciples were eating their meals with unclean hands.
Mark 7:15	Nothing that enters one from outside can defile a person.
Mark 7:19	Jesus declares all foods clean.

Mark 7:27–28	Synophoenician woman outwits Jesus over the meaning of bread.
Mark 8:1–10	Jesus feeds 4,000 starving people from seven loaves and a few fish. Seven baskets of fragments are collected.
Mark 8:14–21	Disciples do not understand the meaning of the multiplication of the loaves and are agitated because they have one mere loaf in the boat.
Mark 9:41	Jesus says: Anyone who gives you a cup of water to drink because you belong to Christ, amen I say to you, will surely not lose his reward.
Mark 9:50	"Salt is good, but if salt becomes insipid, with what will you restore its flavor? Keep salt in yourselves, and you will have peace with one another."
Mark 10:38	Jesus asks James and John: "Can you drink the cup that I drink or be baptized with the baptism with which I am baptized?"
Mark 10:39	James and John say that they can. Jesus agrees.
Mark 11:1–10	Jesus enters Jerusalem on a colt.
Mark 11:12–14	Hungry Jesus curses the fig tree.
Mark 11:15–17	Jesus cleanses the Temple and overturns the seats of those selling doves.
Mark 12:1–12	Jesus' parable about the vineyard and the rebellious tenants.
Mark 12:33	Love of neighbor is worth more than all burnt offerings and sacrifices.
Mark 12:39	Scribes like seats of honor in synagogues and places of honor at banquets.
Mark 13:8	There will be famines.
Mark 14:1	Passover and feast of Unleavened Bread were near.
Mark 14:3–9	Jesus anointed while reclining at table in the house of Simon, the leper.

Mark 14:12-16	Preparation for Passover, mentioned four times.
Mark 14:18	As they reclined at table and were eating, Jesus said: "Amen, I say to you, one of you will betray me, one who is eating with me."
Mark 14:22-26	Words of institution over bread and cup of wine and Jesus' words: "I shall not drink again of the fruit of the vine until the day when I drink it new in God's kingdom."
Mark 14:27	Jesus quotes Scripture: "I will strike the shepherd, and the sheep will be dispersed."
Mark 14:30	Jesus tells Peter that before the cock crows twice he will deny him thrice.
Mark 14:36	Jesus prays: "Take this cup away from me, but not my will but yours."
Mark 14:72	The cock crows after Peter's third denial. He breaks down and weeps.
Mark 15:23	Crucifiers give Jesus wine drugged with myrrh that he does not take.
Mark 15:36	One of the bystanders offers the crucified Jesus wine to drink. [Mark 16:14-18—risen Jesus appears to the Eleven at table and commissions them. If they drink any deadly thing, it will not harm them.]—This is one of the longer endings of Mark. While canonical, it is not part of the authentic ending.

I draw the conclusion from the sheer frequency with which food imagery occurs in Mark's Gospel that it functions as a theme therein. Some of Mark's references to food are quite unique and unexpected. Unexpected, for sure, is the placing of the head of John the Baptist on a food platter. Extraordinary is Jesus' declaration that all foods are clean. Unexpected, also, is the Syrophoenician woman's besting of Jesus over the meaning of bread. But perhaps most unexpected are Mark's references to Jesus' multiplication of loaves for 5,000 people and for 4,000 people followed by Jesus' rebuke of his disciples because they failed to understand the meaning of loaves (Mark 6:34–8:21). It seems that despite being with Jesus the disciples are like the Pharisees and have no understanding (8:21).

There is no space in this book to enter into a detailed discussion of Mark's theological use of Jesus' double multiplication of loaves. Suffice it to say that a possible key to Mark's meaning is to be found in his theological geography, for Mark 6:34–8:21 occurs while Jesus is in Galilee and before he journeys to Jerusalem and explains to his disciples the meaning of his death and resurrection. Once Jesus has been raised, he will precede his disciples to Galilee. See Mark 14:28: "But after I have been raised up, I shall go before you to Galilee." In Galilee once again, this time with the risen Lord Jesus, the disciples will comprehend the meaning of multiplication of loaves as the Bread of Life for Jew and Gentile.

The Theme of Food in Matthew's Gospel

Luke's Gospel has twenty-four chapters. John's Gospel runs to twenty-one chapters. It takes Mark a mere sixteen chapters to narrate his Gospel of Jesus. Matthew covers twenty-eight chapters in telling his story of Jesus. I do not enter into a discussion here of how independent Matthew was in his use of food imagery, since he followed two sources, namely, Mark and Q. [Q mainly consists of sayings material that Matthew and Luke have in common.] Whether he borrowed from Mark and Q, Matthew is responsible for what he put into his Gospel. It is his text that we are studying. In any case, I present the results of my sounding of food imagery in Matthew's Gospel. Again I exhort my readers to do their own homework and not poach on my listing.

Matt 3:4	John's clothing of camel's hair; he eats locusts and wild honey.
Matt 3:6-7	John baptizes with water and calls Pharisees and Sadducees brood of vipers.
Matt 3:8	Produce good fruit as a sign of repentance.

Matt 3:10	Tree that does not bear good fruit will be cut down.
Matt 3:11	I baptize with water; he will baptize with Holy Spirit and fire.
Matt 3:12	He will . . . gather his wheat into his barn.
Matt 3:13–16	John baptizes Jesus.
Matt 3:16	John saw God's Spirit descending like a dove, coming upon him.
Matt 4:3	If you are the Son of God, turn these stones into loaves of bread.
Matt 4:4	One does not live by bread alone, but by every word from God's mouth.
Matt 4:18	Jesus calls fishermen Peter and Andrew.
Matt 4:19	I will make you fishers of men and women.
Matt 4:21	Jesus calls fishermen James and John.
Matt 5:6	Blessed and those who hunger and thirst for righteousness.
Matt 5:13	You are the salt of the earth. . . .
Matt 5:23–24	Leave your [sacrificial] gift on the altar and first be reconciled.
Matt 6:11	Give us today our daily bread.
Matt 6:16–18	When you fast, do not look gloomy like the hypocrites.
Matt 6:25, 31	Do not worry about your life, what you will eat or drink.
Matt 7:6	Do not give what is holy to dogs, or throw your pearls before hogs.
Matt 7:9–10	Which one of you would give his son a stone when asked for a loaf of bread or a snake when asked for a fish?
Matt 7:15–19	By their fruits you will discern the false prophets.
Matt 8:4	The cleansed leper is to offer the gift Moses prescribed.
Matt 8:11–12	Many will come from east and west and will recline with Abraham, Isaac, and Jacob at the

	banquet in the kingdom of heaven, but the children of the kingdom will be driven out into the outer darkness. . . .
Matt 8:15	Simon's mother-in-law serves Jesus.
Matt 8:20	Foxes have dens and birds have nests, but I have nowhere to rest my head.
Matt 8:30–32	Herd of hogs drowned in the sea.
Matt 9:10–11	Jesus and his disciples at table in Matthew's house with many toll collectors and sinners. Pharisees question disciples about Jesus' eating with such people.
Matt 9:14–15	Fasting of John's disciples and Pharisees contrasted with nonfasting of Jesus' disciples.
Matt 9:17	New wine for fresh wineskins.
Matt 9:36	Crowds were like sheep without a shepherd.
Matt 9:38	Harvest is abundant, but laborers few. Ask master for laborers.
Matt 10:6	Go rather to the lost sheep of the house of Israel.
Matt 10:16	I am sending you like sheep in the midst of wolves, so be shrewd as serpents and simple as doves.
Matt 10:29	Are not two sparrows sold for a small coin?
Matt 10:31	You are worth more than many sparrows.
Matt 10:42	Whoever gives only a cup of cold water to one of these little ones. . . .
Matt 11:18	John came neither eating nor drinking and they said: He is possessed by a demon.
Matt 11:19	Son of Man came eating and drinking and they said: Look, he is a glutton and a drunkard, a friend of toll collectors and sinners.
Matt 12:1–8	Jesus defends his disciples who eat heads of grain on the Sabbath.
Matt 12:11–12	Which one of you who has a sheep that falls into a pit on the Sabbath will not take hold of

	it and lift it out? How much more valuable a person is than a sheep?
Matt 12:33	A tree is known by its fruit.
Matt 12:34	You brood of vipers.
Matt 13:1–23	Parable of the sower, seed, soils, and harvest and its interpretation.
Matt 13:24–30	Parable of weeds and wheat.
Matt 13:31–32	Parable of mustard seed.
Matt 13:33–34	Parable of yeast and 40 pounds of wheat flour.
Matt 13:36–43	Interpretation of parable of weeds and wheat.
Matt 13:47–50	Parable of net that catches all kinds of fish.
Matt 14:6	Herod's birthday celebration.
Matt 14:8, 11	John the Baptist's head on a food platter.
Matt 14:13–21	Jesus multiplies 5 loaves of bread and fish for 5,000; 12 baskets full of leftovers.
Matt 15:2	Why do your disciples break the tradition of the elders by not washing their hands before they eat a meal?
Matt 15:11	It is not what enters one's mouth that defiles, but what comes out.
Matt 15:13	Every plant that my heavenly Father has not planted will be uprooted.
Matt 15:20	These (vices) are what defile a person, but to eat with unwashed hands does not defile.
Matt 15:24	Jesus says: I was sent only to the lost sheep of the house of Israel.
Matt 15:26–27	Canaanite woman outwits Jesus by responding: Please, Lord, for even the dogs eat the scraps that fall from the table of their masters.
Matt 15:32–39	Jesus feeds 4,000 from seven loaves. Leftovers fill seven baskets.
Matt 16:5–12	Beware of the leaven of the Pharisees and Sadducees. Disciples are led to understand about the two multiplications of loaves and the leftovers.

Matt 17:15	Boy, who is a lunatic, often falls into water.
Matt 17:27	Peter is to take the first fish he catches. In it he will find a coin worth twice the Temple tax.
Matt 18:12-13	Parable of man who leaves 99 sheep in pursuit of the one lost sheep.
Matt 20:1-16	Generosity of owner of a vineyard to his workers.
Matt 20:22-23	Zebedee's boys will drink from Jesus' cup.
Matt 21:1-7	Jesus enters Jerusalem riding on an ass and a colt.
Matt 21:12	Jesus overturns the seats of those selling doves in the Temple.
Matt 21:18-22	Jesus curses fig tree.
Matt 21:29	In the parable of the two sons (21:28-32) the father asks the first son to work in the vineyard.
Matt 21:33-46	Parable of the vineyard, the trusting master, and the wretched tenants.
Matt 22:1-10	Parable of the wedding feast.
Matt 22:11-14	Guest at wedding feast without a wedding garment.
Matt 23:6	Jesus denounces scribes and Pharisees for their love of places of honor at banquets.
Matt 23:23	Woe to scribes and Pharisees for paying tithes on mint and dill and cumin and neglecting justice, mercy, and loving kindness.
Matt 23:37	Jesus laments: Jerusalem, how many times I yearned to gather your children together as a hen fathers her young under her wings.
Matt 24:7	At the end there will be famines and earthquakes.
Matt 24:38	In the days before the flood at Noah's time they were eating and drinking.
Matt 24:45-51	Faithful steward does not beat up fellow servants and eat and drink with drunkards.

Matt 25:10	In the Parable of the Ten Virgins (25:1-13) the five wise ones go into the wedding feast with the bridegroom.
Matt 25:24, 26	In the parable of the Talents (25:14–30) the master is described as harvesting what he did not plant and gathering where he did not scatter.
Matt 25:35, 37	In the parable of Sheep and Goats (25:31–46): You saw me hungry and fed me and thirsty and you gave me something to drink.
Matt 25:42, 44	In same parable: I was hungry and you gave me no food. I was thirsty and you gave me nothing to drink.
Matt 26:2	Jesus says to his disciples: You know that in two days' time it will be Passover and I will be handed over to be crucified.
Matt 26:8	Jesus is anointed for burial while reclining at table.
Matt 26:17-19	Disciples, at Jesus' instructions, prepare for Passover.
Matt 26:20-25	Jesus reclines at table with the Twelve, and the betrayer dips his hand into the dish with Jesus.
Matt 26:26-29	Jesus' words of institution over bread and cup and his promise that from now on he will not drink the fruit of the vine with them until the day when he drinks it with them new in his Father's kingdom.
Matt 26:31	Jesus sees fulfilled: "I will strike the shepherd, and the sheep of the flock will be dispersed."
Matt 26:34	Peter's denial foretold: Before the cock crows, you will deny me thrice.
Matt 26:39, 42	Jesus will drink the cup that Father has proffered.
Matt 26:74-75	At Peter's third denial the cock crows. Peter withdraws and weeps bitterly.

Matt 27:24	Pilate takes water and wash his hands: "I am innocent of this man's blood."
Matt 27:34	Crucified Jesus does not drink the wine mixed with gall that was offered him.
Matt 27:48	Bystander gives Jesus a sponge soaked in wine.
Matt 27:55	Many women were present, who had followed Jesus from Galilee and had ministered to him.

I count ninety-four instances of food imagery in Matthew's Gospel. The sheer number of occurrences of food imagery in Matthew would seem to qualify for a theme. But if we apply to this material the second criterion of the unexpected, do we find that any instances meet this criterion? I venture to suggest that the instances in Matthew's five blocks of teaching material come closest to the category of the unexpected, for twenty-eight out of the ninety-four instances of food imagery occur in those five blocks. There are nine instances in Matthew 5:3–7:27; five in Matthew 10:5-42; six in Matthew 13:3-53; one in Matthew 18:3-35; and seven in Matthew 24:4–25:46. While this is an impressive array of material, I wonder out loud whether it raises Matthew's use of food imagery to the level of a theme. Put another way, does Matthew's use of food imagery promote his presentation of the significance of Jesus the Messiah? At this reading I would have to suggest that Matthew's use of food imagery is largely incidental to his proclamation of Jesus of Nazareth, who is God with us. Of course, my readers may beg to differ with me, but then they would have to present their reasons and thereby engage Matthew's Gospel in earnest. If this is the result of dissent, long may it live!

Conclusion

Our study of the Gospels of John, Mark, and Matthew have offered us the opportunity to try out our new fishing skills. It has been my pleasure to trawl along with you for the theme of food in these three Gospels. A side benefit of our work together has been the appreciation of how unique Luke's Gospel is, especially with its emphasis on Jesus' symposium meals with Pharisees. While astute readers may drink their way through John's Gospel, they will enjoy eating their way through Luke's Gospel.

Suggested Questions for Reflection

1. After studying Mark's two feeding miracles and the anxiety of Jesus' disciples because they lacked bread, one commentator titled this section in Mark: Full stomachs and hard hearts. Isn't this view of the disciples too harsh? Might any contemporary disciples with full bellies have hard hearts? Does one see better on an empty tummy?

2. Does John's theme of food help you to penetrate more easily into the reality of Jesus? Even though John's Gospel doesn't present Jesus at table with the Pharisees, do you think John's Gospel has much in common with Luke's Gospel? For example, both have the risen Jesus eating with his disciples.

3. Do you think that I have too easily concluded that Matthew does not use food imagery to assist him in showing who Jesus is? How would you assess Matthew's use of food imagery?

Suggestions for Further Reading

Anderson, Janice Capel. "Feminist Criticism: The Dancing Daughter." In Janice Capel Anderson, and Stephen D. Moore, eds., *Mark & Method: New Approaches in Biblical Studies*. Minneapolis: Fortress, 1992, 103–34.

Fowler, Robert M. *Loaves and Fishes: The Function of the Feeding Stories in the Gospel of Mark*. Society of Biblical Literature Dissertation Series 54. Chico: Scholars Press, 1981.

Thurston, Bonnie Bowman. *Preaching Mark*. Minneapolis: Fortress, 2002, 71–95.

Webster, Jane S. *Ingesting Jesus: Eating and Drinking in the Gospel of John*. Society of Biblical Literature Academia Biblica 6. Atlanta: SBL, 2003.

Chapter 7

Food and Women

As we embark on this new chapter, the first thing I ask my readers to do is to check their stereotypes, presuppositions, and cultural expectations. My mother never taught me how to cook. I taught myself, arguing that anyone who can read and take a risk will be able to cook. But when my mother's widowed brother had to cook for himself, he frequently bewailed the fact that he now had to do woman's work. Recently a highly skilled and learned woman had to excuse herself from a meeting we were attending. She told us that she had to go home to cook for her equally learned husband who, although he got home from work ahead of her, could not or would not fight against the stereotype that wives are supposed to cook for husbands. Doctrinal presuppositions may prevent us from seeing that women had leadership positions during New Testament times. While we blithely cite Augustine's words about Mary Magdalene being "The Apostle to the Apostles," we fail to see the implications of his words, for we labor under the impression that only men can be apostles. Even St. John Chrysostom (d. 407), who was most proficient in Greek and a misogynist, had to praise the apostle Junia in his comments on Romans 16:7: "To be an apostle is something great. But to be outstanding among the apostles, just think of what a wondrous song of praise that is. . . . Truly, how great the wisdom of this woman must have been that she was even deemed worthy of the title of apostle."

Chrysostom clearly saw that Junia was an apostle and outstanding among the apostles and not merely held in high regard by male apostles. In what follows I will argue, from a literary point of view, that women disciples were present at Jesus' last earthly meal.

So let us pray the Lord to open our eyes to see five texts anew: Luke 1:46-55; 8:1-3; 10:38-42; 22:14-38; and 24:36-52. I will keep my comments short and meaty and invite discussion and debate.

Two Women Doing Theology and Not Doing the Dishes—Luke 1:39-56

Brigitte Kahl has alerted me to something that is right on the surface of the text of Luke 1:39-56, but that cultural and liturgical presuppositions had prevented me from seeing. Don't we celebrate Mary's Visitation of Elizabeth on May 31 as a feast whose opening prayer is: "Eternal Father, you inspired the Virgin Mary, mother of your Son, to visit Elizabeth and assist her in her need. . . ."? Isn't that how we read this passage, that Mary is assisting Elizabeth in her need by doing domestic chores? Mary will be doing the cooking, the dishes, and the laundry. Yet Luke says not a single word about these activities. If that were his point, he won't have Mary depart just when Elizabeth needed her most, at the time of the birth of John. Read very carefully what Luke says: "Mary remained with Elizabeth about three months and then returned to her home. When the time arrived for Elizabeth to have her child, she gave birth to a son."

The words of Elizabeth and Mary are overtures to Luke's Gospel and set the stage for what is to follow. Mary is indeed "the mother of Elizabeth's and the world's Lord." Elizabeth praises Mary for her belief and thus sets the tone for the picture that Luke will paint of Mary in Luke–Acts. Mary is the one who will ponder the events of Jesus' early years in her heart (2:19, 51). Through her heart the sword of discernment will pass, as she decides for or against belief in her son as Lord (2:35).

In the Upper Room, Mary, along with the twelve apostles and a large group numbering 120, will await her Lord's promised Holy Spirit (Acts 1:14-15). El Greco's painting of Pentecost in the Museo del Prado in Madrid, Spain, comes very close to Luke's intention as he features Mary, not Peter, in the center of his majestic rendition of the birth of the church through the gift of the Holy Spirit as fiery tongues. No pots and pans for Elizabeth, for what many have said about her is true: She is a prophet, speaking words of truth, doing theology.

Mary's song of praise, traditionally called the *Magnificat* (1:46-55), has become a canticle at Vespers. But in that form it is separated from its literary and theological context in Luke's Gospel. From our perspective verse 53 is vitally important: "The hungry God has filled with good things, and the rich God has sent away empty." Notice the contrast "hungry-rich." This verse in Mary's overture sets up an expectation of what God will do in Jesus' ministry. Luke's beatitudes and woes express this expectation in a slightly different way: "Blessed are you who are now hungry, for you will be satiated" (6:20). "Woe to you who are filled now, for you will be hungry" (6:25). It seems that Jesus' table fellowship with sinners and toll collectors, who have been starved by Jewish religious leaders, is a fulfillment of what Mary's *Magnificat* anticipates. In his gifts of bread and fish, Jesus will provide food for 5,000 hungry people (9:10-17). At his last earthly meal he will institute food and drink for the world's needy (22:14-38). At least two of Luke's parables address the situation of those who are rich unto themselves and neglect the needy in the community (12:13-21; 16:19-31). In the latter parable there is a reversal of situations, as Lazarus, who was starved in this life, enjoys a choice place at the eternal banquet with Abraham while the rich man, who daily dined sumptuously cannot even get a drop of water to cool his hot thirst.

Let me repeat myself. You will look in vain in Luke 1:38-56 for a picture of Mary at the hearth or washtub. She and Elizabeth are prophets who do theology, not windows or dishes.

Mary Magdalene, Joanna, and Susanna Accompany Jesus—Luke 8:1-3

This passage, unique to Luke, is one that the Lectionary tramples underfoot, since it links it to Jesus' more familiar parable of the sower. I make a number of points, some of which are technical.

First is my translation of the passage reflecting the Greek that has one long sentence held together by "and" followed by "and," etc.

> Soon afterwards Jesus was going through cities and villages, proclaiming and bringing the good news of the kingdom of God, and the Twelve with him, and some women who had been cured of evil spirits and infirmities, Mary, called Magdalene, from whom seven demons had gone out, and Joanna, the wife of Herod's steward, Chuza, and Susanna, and many others, who were serving them out of their financial resources.

Since this sentence of three verses is so long, readers have a tendency to chunk it into bite-sized pieces. Before we do that, however, I offer some grammatical comments. First, seven is a number that means "completeness." Thus, Mary Magdalene has been thoroughly cured of an illness and is not to be considered a consummate sinner, as various legends make her. Second, the Greek verb behind "were serving them" is *diēkonoun*, which in Luke's Gospel generally is used of bringing food to a person. However, Acts and other New Testament texts retain its more basic meaning of "go between." For even those who serve food to others go between the kitchen and the table. I give two NT examples. Phoebe, who is a *diakonos* of the church at Cenchreae, is hardly a waitress in that church (Romans 16:1). Also in Philemon 13, Paul refers to Onesimus as one who served him in his imprisonment for the Gospel. Onesimus was not some sort of butler for the imprisoned Paul, but was Paul's go-between or messenger in the interests of the Gospel. Third, if we follow certain Greek manuscripts and read "them" in 8:3, who are they? Are the women providing for the men, that is, Jesus and the

Twelve? Or are the "many other women" serving Jesus, the Twelve, Mary Magdalene, Joanna, and Susanna? That is, are the three named women part of the team that proclaims the Gospel of the kingdom of God? Fourth, if we follow those Greek manuscripts that are noted in the NRSV footnote and read "him," then we may legitimately take *diēkonoun* in its basic sense of "go-between" or as messengers. That is, these women went on mission for Jesus or were messengers.

The fifth and final grammatical point deserves a paragraph of its own. Luke 8:1-3 is what is called "a summary passage." I use Maria Anicia Co's definition: "a relatively independent and concise narrative statement that describes a prolonged situation or portrays an event as happening repeatedly within an indefinite period of time" (56–57). The implications of Luke 8:1-3 as a summary are vast. The women of Luke 8:1-3 are present with Jesus even when Luke does not specifically mention them. That such is the case is made clear in Luke 24:6-8. In that passage Luke says that the women remember the words of Jesus that he spoke to them in Galilee. Now in Luke 8:22 and 18:33-34, the closest parallels to the wording of Luke 24:7, there is no specific mention of the presence of women. Thus, Luke 24:6-8 is a flashback or completing analepsis in narrative analysis. As we will see later in this chapter, the implications of calling Luke 8:1-3 a summary have vast implications for resolving the question of who was present at Jesus' last earthly meal.

Granted these grammatical considerations, how do we chunk this passage and make sense of it? On one level, this passage talks about the inclusive nature of discipleship. Both men and women are disciples. Joanna is wife of Chuza, who managed Herod's estates, and thus seems to have been a woman of means and prominence. In that case one can argue that Jesus' Gospel breaks down economic and class divisions, too. On another level, this passage, especially its use of the verb "were serving," may imply more than that the women were a traveling catering service for the men. They may have been messengers for Jesus. Marianne Sawicki has provided a somewhat speculative indication of how Mary Magdalene as a businesswoman was Jesus' messenger, while Richard Bauckham has provided the same for Joanna.

Two Good Sisters Serve the Lord—Luke 10:38-42

Luke 10:38-42 has such a long history of interpretation, especially in popular preaching, that it may be hard to read the text afresh. Nonetheless, let's try our hand.

I read this text about two good sisters in the light of its total context in Luke's Gospel. In a Gospel that stresses hospitality, this story is a prime example, for Martha welcomes weary Jesus and his disciples into her home. She gives a positive example of how to receive a missionary in accordance with the instructions of Luke 10:8 and provides a counter to the negative example of those Samaritans who would not welcome Jesus (9:53). Like Zacchaeus in 19:6 she is happy to welcome the Lord into her home. It seems reasonable to assume that such an offer of hospitality would include a meal or table fellowship.

The second context in Luke's Gospel is Luke's account of how Jesus conducted himself at table. At each table Jesus has a word to say to the host or to those who recline with him at table. During the great banquet that Levi hosts, Jesus defends his eating and drinking with toll collectors and sinners and tries to teach the Pharisees and their scribes the meaning of mercy (5:27-32). In 7:36-50 Jesus takes Simon to task for his lack of hospitality to him and praises the generosity of the forgiven woman sinner. In 11:37-54 Jesus teaches the Pharisees and scribes the true meaning of ritual purity. In 14:1-24 Jesus teaches his Pharisee host and table companions the meaning of humility and challenges them to invite the poor, maimed, crippled, and blind to their banquets. At his last earthly meal Jesus must correct his own disciples as they squabble about who is first. Even in 24:13-35 Jesus must correct his two disciples on the road to Emmaus and in anticipation of their meal together for their foolishness and lazy hearts. It is no real objection to say that Simon doesn't speak in 7:36-50 or the Pharisee in 11:37-54, for Jesus reads what they are saying in their very hearts. Jesus' criticism of Martha's anxiety is part and parcel of Luke's table fellowship style. Her anxiety may impede her from doing her job well. Recall 8:14 that tells of the seed or word that fell among thorns. Such seeds are choked by "the anxieties and riches and pleasures of life and fail to produce mature fruit." A final point: As we read Luke's stories of Jesus at table, with whom do we readers identify? It seems to me that it is only with 10:38-42 that we tend to identify with one of the sisters, whereas in the other table fellowship stories we identify with Jesus. What I am proposing is that we also identify with Jesus in 10:38-42. Try it. You may like it.

Having set the context for this story, I now focus on the word "serving" that occurs twice in 10:40. If you recall our discussion just a minute ago of this word in our consideration of Luke 8:3, you may realize that this word may refer to Martha's ministerial activity. She is anxious that Mary join her in that work. But even if we take "serving" in that meaning, the emphasis of the passage is not on the contrast between contemplation and action, but on being anxious to the degree of missing the boat.

In the reading of Luke 10:38-42 that I am proposing both sisters are good. As in his other occasions at table, Jesus does not condemn, but correct. When Jesus is the guest, all eyes must be on him. He is the one thing necessary.

Jesus Gives Life to Transgressors—Luke 22:14-38

I begin my treatment of this very important passage by offering some general observations. After that, I will comment on the five sections that comprise this passage.

While of great significance, Jesus' words of institution over the bread and wine are not the center of attention in this passage. That is, we readers should not gallop to 22:19-20 and think that by understanding these two verses we have grasped all of 22:14–38. This meal is the last symposium meal in a sequence of meals celebrated by Jesus, "glutton and drunkard, friend of toll collectors and sinners." When the Lukan Jesus says in 22:19: Do *this* in memory of me, he is not just referring to the Passover meal he is celebrating with his male and female disciples, but to all the meals he has celebrated in his ministry. Check back to Luke 5:27–32, which depicts Jesus' meal with Levi and other toll collectors and sinners and records Jesus' defense of his disciples' eating with people of such ilk. Recall 7:36–50 where prophet Jesus chides Simon for not extending hospitality to him and forgives the sins of a generous woman. Luke 9:10–17 portrays Jesus as Lord of life as he provides abundant food for 5,000 people, all of whose eyes are fixed on him. In 10:38–42 Martha and Mary offer hospitality to Jesus and are challenged to center their lives on him, the one thing necessary. Luke 11:37–53 presents Jesus again at table with religious leaders, challenging them for their lack of justice and teaching them that true ritual purity is accomplished through alms for the poor. In Luke 14:1–24 Jesus once again chides the religious leaders for seeking first places at symposium meals and for not inviting the unfortunate to their tables of plenty. Luke 19:1–10 is the high point of Jesus' association with toll collectors. Despite the murmurings of the bystanders, Jesus goes to dine with Zacchaeus, a rich, chief tax collector who gives half of his possessions to the poor. When Jesus says: Do this in memory of me, he is globally referring to his table fellowship with the recently converted, sinners, and toll collectors. It should not surprise us that a number of the features we noted in Jesus' earlier meals recur at his last earthly meal, for example, controversy.

Besides displaying the form of a symposium meal, Jesus' final earthly meal also bears traces of what is technically called a Farewell Discourse. Jesus, like illustrious people in Israel's history, speaks about the meaning of life with God and tells his followers how to walk in his footsteps. A fine example of the literary form of a Farewell Discourse occurs in "The Testament of Joseph" in the intertestamental book called *The Testaments of the Twelve Patriarchs.* Joseph is at death's door and beckons his children and relatives to him. His life of fidelity to God becomes a model for them as Joseph recalls the highlights of his life as detailed in Genesis. He tells of his chastity in the face of the temptations to adultery from Pharaoh's wife and of his merciful reconciliation with his brothers who had sold him into slavery. Joseph, who had seemed doomed to death and separated from his family and people, was rescued by God and had become the savior of people by providing them with food. Through his story of Joseph the author exhorts his readers to similar fidelity to God in the midst of adversity and trial. As we will see, Jesus also bequeaths to his disciples an example of fidelity to God despite trials and gives them an example of his lifestyle of serving others rather than serving self.

Preparation for Us Readers—Luke 22:1-13

My comments on Luke 22:1-13 are geared to prepare us to read Luke's account of Jesus' last earthly meal. Jesus is in charge. Although Judas betrays Jesus, Jesus gives directions to Peter and John to make preparations for their eating of the Passover (22:8). The meal Jesus will eat is a celebrative one that commemorates the Exodus of the Jews from the slavery of Egypt through God's liberating power. Jesus does not eat this meal with family, but with his female and male disciples. Leonardo da Vinci's mural of the *Last Supper,* while it may be great art and may have influenced millions of people, does not accurately portray Luke's painting of Jesus' last earthly meal. Why? To start with the most obvious, Jesus and his disciples are reclining at table, not sitting (22:14). I continue with what I mentioned above in our consideration of Luke 8:1-3, which is commonly held to be a summary or "a relatively independent and concise narrative statement that describes a prolonged situation or portrays an event as happening repeatedly within an indefinite period of time." That is, even if a particular text such as Jesus' last earthly meal does not explicitly indicate that women were present, Luke implies that they were present. Further, Luke has not made it crystal clear that the only participants at his description of Jesus' last earthly meal are the Twelve or the apostles. His terminology fluctuates in 22:1-38: Judas, one of the Twelve (22:3; see also 22:30, 47); apostles (22:14); disciples (22:11; see also 22:39, 45); "brothers" (22:32 where brothers equals "disciples"). To this obvious fluctuation I add the subtle one that occurs in 22:35-36. The curious and diligent reader will discover that 22:35-36 is not a reference to the sending out of the Twelve (9:1-6), but to the sending out of the seventy other disciples (10:1-16). As we will see in what follows, especially on 22:21-29, Luke, at the very least, is reading his own community of men and women back into Jesus' last earthly meal. Need I remind my readers that Luke is not writing history, but theology, and doing theology through such literary means as a symposium meal and a farewell discourse?

Jesus Shares His Life with Others Through Bread and Wine—Luke 22:14-20

Just as a Jewish father interpreted the components of the Passover meal, so too does Jesus. But Jesus does not interpret the lamb or the bitter herbs, but just the abundant wine and the bread. Luke 22:15-18 contains Jesus' interpretation of a cup of Passover wine in terms of God's eschatological banquet. Isaiah 25:6 seems to be on the horizon where Isaiah depicts God's final victory: "On this mountain the Lord of hosts will provide for all peoples a feast of rich food and choice wines, juicy, rich food and pure, choice wines." Luke 22:19-20, which reflects the most reliable Greek manuscripts, conveys Jesus' interpretation of Passover bread and wine with reference to his salvific death that inaugurates a new covenant. Whilst in the Passover liturgy the father distributed the bread and wine as symbols of God's and his provision for his family, Jesus now provides not bread and wine, but his very self for his brothers and sisters. Jesus replaces the Passover meal with another meal that liberates from enslaving forces and is a foretaste of the heavenly banquet. Yet I must remind my readers that this meal should not be isolated or separated from all the previous meals that Jesus enjoyed, especially those with sinners. Even if you tend to forget, Luke's very next section will jolt you back to attention.

Who among the Brothers and Sisters Might Betray Jesus Now?—Luke 22:21-23

Professor Arthur Vööbus has taught me not to follow those translations that try to historicize 22:21-23. If Luke wanted to say "Judas," he could have. If Luke wanted to say "woe to that man," he could have, but he didn't. He said: "Woe to that person." Luke, a master of food symbolism, uses this passage to draw his readers into the meaning of Jesus' last earthly meal for themselves. Are Luke's readers, are we readers going to continue Jesus' type of eating and drinking or are we going to betray him? Could Jesus be eating his last earthly meal with sinners?

A Controversy at Jesus' Final Earthly Meal— Luke 22:24-30

Luke continues his actualization of the meaning of Jesus' last earthly meal by inserting a controversy over greatness into it. In Matthew 20:24-28 and Mark 10:41-45 this argument among the disciples occurs during Jesus' journey to Jerusalem. As Luke does his theology, this argument fits better at Jesus' last earthly meal. In doing so, Luke follows the symposium tradition that often portrayed squabbles among the learned people reclining at table. Jesus corrects his disciples by providing them with his example of serving at table. On a profound level it is true that Jesus is serving his disciples at table by giving them food and drink. Readers can profitably contrast Jesus' lifestyle with that of the religious leaders who seek places of honor at table (14:7; 20:46) and with that of the rich man who feasted daily in a sumptuous manner and cared nothing for those in need who were at his door (16:19-31). If we judge the disciples' behavior in jockeying for positions of honor as sinful, might we include this meal among those that Jesus celebrated with sinners?

Jesus Protects Peter the Sinner and Predicts Changing Times—Luke 22:31-38

In chapter three we devoted some time to Luke's painting of Peter the sinner. Now I remind my readers that Peter, who will shortly sin by denying Jesus, is at what we have traditionally called the Last Supper. Luke is surely depicting Jesus eating and drinking with transgressors to the end. But amidst all these sinners stands the Lord Jesus who says to Simon Peter: "I have prayed that your own faith may not fail" (22:32). As we know from the rest of Luke's Gospel and from his Acts of the Apostles, the prayer of Jesus the Intercessor has been effective.

When I led a discussion of Luke 22:14-38 in a recent continuing education class, a participant said that his church used to be agitated because of the abundant wine enjoyed at Jesus' Last Supper. That's no longer a problem, he said, and added that the church's current problem is the presence of two swords (see 22:38). Well, his church is in good company, for those two swords and their use in 22:49-50 continue to agitate commentators and church people. Suffice it to say that Jesus uses metaphorical language in 22:35-38 to detail the changing times that will enwrap his disciples after his death. That is, sword seems to be a symbol for crisis. I paraphrase 22:36: Sell your treasured cloak upon which you depend for warmth and buy yourself a heap of trouble.

Women Disciples Eat with Risen Jesus and Are Commissioned—Luke 24:36-52

Rather than just repeat what I said above about Luke 8:1-3 and 22:14-38 and the presence of women disciples during Jesus' ministry and at his last earthly meal, I move to a fresh perspective.

When Luke writes "the Eleven and all the rest" (24:9) and "the Eleven and those with them" (24:33), is he referring simply to male disciples or to both women and men? I follow a number of eminent commentators in taking "all the rest" to refer to an unspecified number of male and female Galilean disciples. The risen Lord Jesus opens their minds to understand all of Scripture (24:44-45), as they move from doubt to belief (24:41).

If we think of Luke 24:41-43 at all, we may think it somewhat strange that the risen Lord Jesus eats a piece of broiled fish in the presence of his male and female disciples. Granted an apologetic note to display the reality of Jesus' bodily resurrection, this passage should not be read in our cultural context of eating alone. As social scientific critics have been telling us for years now, people in the Mediterranean basin didn't eat by themselves. So even though Luke does not specifically say that Jesus ate a fish dinner with his male and female disciples, such is the gist of 24:41-43. If any of my readers may have any doubts, I refer them to what Peter says: "This man God raised on the third day and granted that he be visible, not to all the people, but to us, the witnesses chosen by God in advance, who ate and drank with him after he rose from the dead" (Acts 10:39-40). Now if you remember how poorly Jesus' disciples conducted themselves at his last earthly meal, might 24:41-43 give just a hint of Jesus' reconciliation with those men and women who were present with him at his Last Supper? But not only does the risen Lord Jesus grant his fallible disciples forgiveness at a meal, he also commissions these men and women (24:36-49). There is sufficient evidence at that time that Jewish women could be witnesses.

Conclusion

Luke has much to say about women disciples and does so through the theme of food. Suffice it to say that the women, beginning with Jesus' own mother, Mary, are not consigned to fussing about provisions.

Suggested Questions for Reflection

1. Dan Brown's novel, *The Da Vinci Code*, has been on the best-seller lists for years, has sold over millions upon millions of copies in hardback, and has caused some authors to rush to print to assault its mistakes. Knowledge of "the code" allows one to see that Mary Magdalene is sitting next to Christ at the Last Supper. Does one really need "the da Vinci code" to learn that women were present with Jesus when he ate his final earthly meal? What might be some implications of this fact?

2. Has my explanation of Luke 10:38-42 helped you get a handle on this story of hospitality? How good/bad was the last sermon you heard preached on this text? Did the preacher stress the role of Christ in this story? How would you preach a homily on this passage?

3. In what ways is Luke 22:14-38 a recapitulation of all the meals that Jesus has shared with people during his earthly life? To get your mind around this question, you might want to compare Luke's version of events with the far shorter ones of Matthew and Mark.

Suggestions for Further Reading

Bauckham, Richard. *Gospel Women: Studies of Named Women in the Gospel.* Grand Rapids, MI: Eerdmans, 2002.

Brumberg-Kraus, Jonathan. "'Not by Bread Alone . . . ': The Ritual-ization of Food and Table Talk in the Passover *Seder* and in the Last Supper," *Semeia* 86 (1999) 165–91.

Co, Maria Anicia. "The Major Summaries in Acts: Acts 2,42-47; 4,32-35; 5,12-16: Linguistic and Literary Relationships," *Ephemerides theologicae lovanienses* 68 (1992) 49–85.

Kahl, Brigette. "Reading Luke Against Luke: Non-Uniformity of Text, Hermeneutics of Conspiracy and 'the Scriptural Principle.'" In Amy-Jill Levine, ed., *A Feminist Companion to Luke.* London: Sheffield Academic Press, 2002, 70–88.

Karris, Robert J. *Prayer and the New Testament: Jesus and His Communities at Prayer*. New York: Crossroad, 2000, 44–51.

———. "Women and Discipleship in Luke." In Amy-Jill Levine, ed., *A Feminist Companion to Luke*. London: Sheffield Academic Press, 2002, 23–43. Originally published in *Catholic Biblical Quarterly* 56 (1994) 1–20.

Sawicki, Marianne. *Crossing Galilee: Architectures of Contact in the Occupied Land of Jesus*. Harrisburg, PA: Trinity Press International, 2000.

Chapter 8

Eating Is a Serious and Dangerous, but Also a Joyful Business

While waiting my turn for drilling, I happened to notice that my dentist had the latest issue of *Reader's Digest*. Its cover story was "How Safe Is Our Food?" Yes, we must be careful of food poisoning in various forms and are subject to warnings each Thanksgiving about how to prepare a delicious and safe turkey. When you see men and women dressed to the nines for a wedding or festive banquet, you come to the quick realization that eating is also a serious business. A suit or dress for such an occasion might well cost more than the food. In this concluding chapter I want to take a serious look at Jesus' eating under the rubrics of Jesus and his disciples. I hope my readers will excuse me for adding a third ingredient to eating as a serious and dangerous business. A refrain in Luke 15 taught me the necessity of this ingredient. It is joy.

Jesus

Twenty years ago I introduced two statements. In Luke's Gospel Jesus is either going to a meal, at a meal, or coming from a meal. In Luke's Gospel Jesus got himself killed because of the way he ate. I am happy to say that these two statements have entered into the mainstream of Lukan scholarship. If you have learned anything from this book, it is that Jesus loves to eat and gets himself in deep trouble with the religious leaders of his day because of his eating habits, especially his eating with toll collectors and sinners. Let us pause with these statements and ponder some of their theological implications. If Jesus is the Son of God made flesh, then his incarnation means eating and drinking, and the vulnerability, dependence, and humility that are integral to the human condition of consuming food. Some authors are even going so far as to commend that their readers contemplate Jesus using the restroom, for the elimination of waste follows from sustaining life by eating and drinking. Jesus was one of us in all things but sin.

Jesus enjoys an inclusive table, be it with toll collectors, sinners, men, women, hostile religious leaders, and even fallible disciples. He shares his last earthly meal with a disciple who will betray him, with disciples who yearn for positions of power, and with Peter who will deny him. After his resurrection, Jesus the Lord brings to the table of reconciliation the two disciples who had abandoned his way and are journeying away from Jerusalem to Emmaus. As Jesus gathers these folks around him at table, it is hard not to think of him enjoying himself. If my readers will excuse me from smuggling John 21 into my discussion of Luke, I state that the best rendition of a joyous Jesus is "The Risen Christ by the Sea" by Jack Jewell and available at www. joyfulnoise.com. Jesus is inviting his disciples to enjoy the fish dinner he has prepared for them. If my readers prefer to get inside the joy of an inclusive table by means of a movie, I recommend *Babette's Feast* and include pertinent data in "Suggestions for Further Reading" at the end of this chapter.

But Jesus not only loves to break bread with the sinners of this world, he also provides food. Luke frequently makes this point. Although I didn't accentuate this passage in my earlier chapters, Luke 2:7 starts Luke's presentation of Jesus in a unique way: He is in a manger. Luke's threefold note of manger indicates that it is important to him (2:7, 12, 16). Just as a manger is a place for food, so too is Jesus food. As we have seen, Jesus provides food for 5,000 banqueters who have abundant food to sustain their lives (9:10-17). At his final earthly meal Jesus bequeaths to his male and female disciples the gift of his Body and Blood in the Eucharist (22:14-38).

Jesus' Disciples, Then and Now

Even though I separate this section from the previous one about Jesus, I realize that there will of necessity be overlapping. In our very first chapter we saw that it was very likely that Jesus, along with most people of his time, ate very little meat. Thus, his lifestyle was largely vegetarian. Stephen H. Webb's book *Good Eating* explores this theme in depth. For example, did you ever stop to think that the Eucharist, in contrast to a Passover Seder meal, is a vegetarian meal? Webb helpfully points to a long Christian tradition of fasting and abstaining from meat.

The phrase "women and food" quickly passes over to "women in ministry." In my last chapter I championed the viewpoint that Luke presents women in a favorable light. He didn't have to mention the women who journeyed with Jesus, who ate with him at his final earthly meal, were at the cross, were the first witnesses of his resurrection, and ate with him at his meal of reconciliation with his disciples after his resurrection. But Luke narrated those events in his Gospel for future generations to make sense of and not hide behind a statue someplace. Luke probably contributed to the opinion of the Roman Catholic Church's Pontifical Biblical Commission in 1976 that scriptural grounds alone are not enough to exclude the possibility of ordaining women.

Contemporary sociological and anthropological studies raise issues about women and food that may compel us to look at Luke's Gospel in a different way. These studies ask: Why are women, not men, burdened with cooking? Why are women compelled to be a certain weight when men can balloon? When food is so abundant and varied, why are so many people, especially women, on diets? Why are there eating disorders, especially among women who select, prepare, and serve food? At first blush these questions seem to be too contemporary to be applied to Luke's time when most people were of modest means and thus had little access to great quantities of food. Yet these questions do force us to examine our stereotypes. We saw some of these stereotypes in play when we investigated the meaning of "the serving" of Mary Magdalene, Joanna, Susanna, and many other women in Luke 8:1-3 and Martha in 10:38-42.

The issue of who controls food is sometimes explicit in Luke's Gospel, but most often one has to read between the lines to detect it. The Jewish religious leaders control their food, tithe it, prepare it properly, prepare themselves by ritual washings to eat it properly, and share it with people like themselves. In brief, they control who eats with them and with whom they eat. If we accept the common scholarly model that Jesus lived in a peasant society, then it follows that the few people at the top of the social and political pyramid controlled not only taxes but also food. They ate very well. Take the Emperor Vitellius, for example, who was a notorious glutton. Through his use of purgatives he was able to feast three or four times a day. Each meal cost no less than $400,000. The Roman historian Suetonius tells us that at one of these banquets there were 2,000 of the choicest fish, 7,000 birds, etc., etc. When Luke mentions Caesar Augustus before he narrates that the newborn Jesus is laid in a manger, an enlightened reader can begin to smell the difference between the kinds of food each provided. Today our government tries to present a food pyramid to keep the nation healthy. I've even seen them in grade school cafeterias. But as Marion Nestle and others have shown, the government's food pyramid is largely window dressing. For the government provides mere millions to advertise its pyramid while the food industry spends billions to topple the pyramid and turn a big profit for its shareholders. Who really controls our food?

As we disciples reflect upon the question of who controls food, we turn to our Lord who was criticized for being the friend of sinners and toll collectors and ask whether contemporary churches provide an inclusive table. Who is prevented from receiving the Eucharist and for what reasons? Francis J. Moloney provides us with much food for thought on this subject in his book, whose title highlights the Eucharist as food for a broken, not a spiritually robust people: *A Body Broken for a Broken People.*

Disciples who follow the Jesus of Luke's Gospel do not look forward to the beatific vision in heaven, but to full participation at the delights of the heavenly banquet. At that time God's kingdom will have come, and Jesus will recline at table with his disciples to drink of the fruit of the vine (22:18). The Irish St. Brigit teaches us all to follow the Lord of the Banquet and to look forward to rich heavenly food and abundant heavenly drink. Her prayer about inclusive table fellowship is famous and has been set to music by Samuel Barber as number four of his "Hermit Songs":

> I would like to have the men of heaven in my house with vats of good cheer laid out for them. I would like to have the three Marys (of Nazareth, of Bethany, and of Magdala), for their fame is so great. I would like men and women from every corner of heaven. I would like them to be cheerful in their drinking. I would love to have Jesus reclining here among them. I would like a great lake of beer for the King of Kings. I would delight in watching the family of heaven drinking it through all eternity.

I conclude with a line from the prayer that we disciples pray so frequently. In the Lord's Prayer we voice our petition: Give us each day our daily bread. In an earlier chapter we explored very briefly the humility, faith, and acknowledgment of dependence involved in this simple petition. I also noted its communal nature, as we depend on others for our food and share our food with others. Perhaps the implementation of our side of this prayer is the biggest single obligation for United States Christians today. I refer interested readers to L. Shannon Jung's book *Food for Life,* whose appendices provide video and educational resources. Among these resources is Bread for the World at www.bread.org. At the end of his book, Jung points to the terrifying implications of setting a truly inclusive table and of sharing our food equitably. Such activities will hit us where it truly hurts—in our stomachs. For we would have to fast and abstain from the abundant and varied food we have come to deem our right. But our sacrifice would lead to life for millions who are starving in the United States and around the world. See www.foodforthepoor.org.

Conclusion

While Luke may not be able to lay claim to all the challenges that a contemporary theology of food puts on our plates, he has surely contributed significantly to them. Or rather, the Jesus whose Gospel he narrates is the one responsible. Some time back a confrere gave me a small bronze plaque of St. Luke. It is an attractive, but busy plaque. In the far right corner there is an easel, since a phase of tradition called Luke an artist. In the near right corner is a sacrificial ox, since tradition holds that the ox represents compassion and that Luke pictures a truly compassionate Christ. In the left center is Luke intent on writing his Gospel. In the top far left is the physician's symbol of a snake on a pole, since tradition maintains that Luke was a physician. At the risk of cluttering the present busy symbolism of this plaque, I would place a loaf of bread and a jug of wine just in front of Luke's writing table and put a big smile on Luke's face. You, the readers who have stayed the course with me, can determine whether the loaf of bread should be made of finest wheat flour or of coarse barley. In any case, as we have learned, it's not there for show, but for sharing.

Suggested Questions for Reflection

1. Think of the thousands of artistic renditions of the Virgin Mary. Is she slim or sturdy? Is Mary Magdalene painted as an anorexic and thin woman? Which Mary do you prefer? Which Mary of Magdala do you prefer? Why?

2. Who controls food in your family, community, parish, state, and nation? How do you judge whether those in charge of food are doing a good job?

3. In what ways could you and yours be better followers of Christ, who enjoyed an inclusive table? Should you be more inclusive at the Eucharist? Does your form of worship exclude certain people?

Suggestions for Further Reading

Adams, Carol J. *The Sexual Politics of Meat: A Feminist-Vegetarian Critical Theory*. Tenth Anniversary Edition. New York: Continuum, 2000.

Counihan, Carole M. *The Anthropology of Food and Body: Gender, Meaning, and Power*. New York/London: Routledge, 1999.

Jung, L. Shannon. *Food for Life: The Spirituality and Ethics of Eating*. Minneapolis: Fortress, 2004.

Lelwica, Michelle Mary. *Starving for Salvation: The Spiritual Dimensions of Eating Problems among American Girls and Women*. New York: Oxford University Press, 1999.

Moloney, Francis J. *A Body Broken for a Broken People: Eucharist in the New Testament*. Revised edition. Peabody, MA: Hendrickson, 1997.

Nestle, Marion. *Food Politics: How the Food Industry Influences Nutrition and Health*. Berkeley, CA: University of California Press, 2002.

Scapp, Ron and Brian Seitz, ed. *Eating Culture*. Albany, NY: State University of New York Press, 1998.

Schlosser, Eric. *Fast Food Nation: The Dark Side of the All-American Meal*. Boston: Houghton Mifflin, 2001.

Webb, Stephen H. *Good Eating*. The Christian Practice of Everyday Life. Grand Rapids, MI: Brazos Press, 2001.

Witt, Doris. *Black Hunger: Food and the Politics of U.S. Identity*. New York: Oxford University Press, 1999.

Babette's Feast, 1989 DVD, World Films.

"Babette's Feast," in Isak Dinesen, *Anecdotes of Destiny and Ehrengard*. New York: Vintage International, 1975, 19–59.

"*Babette's Feast* and Shaming the Poor in Corinth," in Robert Jewett, *Saint Paul Returns to the Movies: Triumph over Shame*. Grand Rapids, MI: Eerdmans, 1999, 38–51.

Keller, Marie Noël. "Eucharist as Table Fellowship," *The Bible Today* 42 (1) (January 2004) 36–42.

Wright, Wendy M. "Babette's Feast: A Religious Film," *Journal of Religion and Film* 1 (2) (October 1997) 1–8.

Selected Bibliography

I list books that I have found helpful and am happy to include titles that deal with food, but do not directly pertain to the study of the New Testament.

Beardsworth, Alan, and Teresa Keil. *Sociology on the Menu*. London: Routledge, 1997.

Bober, Phyllis Pray. *Art, Culture, and Cuisine: Ancient and Medieval Gastronomy*. Chicago: University of Chicago Press, 1999.

Brumberg Kraus, Jonathan. "Symposium Scenes in Luke's Gospel with Special Attention to the Last Supper." Nashville: Vanderbilt University PH.D dissertation, 1991.

Bryne, Brendan. *The Hospitality of God: A Reading of Luke's Gospel*. Collegeville: Liturgical Press, 2000.

Caplan, Pat. *Feasts, Fasts, Famine: Food for Thought*. Berg Occasional Papers in Anthropology 2. Oxford: Berg, 1994.

Corti, Gianluigi. *Amico dei peccatori: Amicizia e perdono del Vangelo di Luca*. Milan: Paoline, 2004

Counihan, Carole, and Penny Van Esterik, eds. *Food and Culture: A Reader*. London: Routledge, 1997.

Dalby, Andrew. *Food in the Ancient World from A to Z*. London: Routledge, 2003.

Davidson, Alan. *Oxford Companion to Food*. New York: Oxford University Press, 1999.

Food: A Culinary History from Antiquity to the Present. Under the direction of Jean-Louis Flandrin and Massimo Montanari. New York: Columbia University Press, 1999.

Garnsey, Peter. *Food and Society in Classical Antiquity*. Key Themes in Ancient History. Cambridge: Cambridge University Press, 1999.

Gowers, Emily. *The Loaded Table: Representations of Food in Roman Literature*. Oxford: Clarendon, 1993.

Hamel, Gildas. *Poverty and Charity in Roman Palestine, First Three Centuries*. University of California Publications: Near Eastern Studies 23. Berkeley: University of California Press, 1990.

Heil, John Paul. *The Meal Scenes in Luke-Acts: An Audience-Oriented Approach*. Society of Biblical Literature Monograph Series 52. Atlanta: SBL, 1999.

Koenig, John. *New Testament Hospitality: Partnership with Strangers as Promise and Mission*. Overtures to Biblical Theology 17. Philadelphia: Fortress, 1985.

Koenig, John. *The Feast of the World's Redemption: Eucharistic Origins and Christian Mission*. Harrisburg, PA: Trinity Press International, 2000.

Korsmeyer, Carolyn. *Making Sense of Taste: Food & Philosophy*. Ithaca: Cornell University Press, 1999.

LaVerdiere, Eugene. *Dining in the Kingdom of God: The Origin of the Eucharist according to Luke*. Chicago: Liturgy Training Publications, 1999.

Levenstein, Harvey A. *Revolution at the Table: The Transformation of the American Diet*. New York: Oxford University Press, 1988.

―――. *Paradox of Plenty: A Social History of Eating in Modern America*. New York: Oxford University Press, 1993.

Montanari, Massimo. *The Culture of Food*. Cambridge: Blackwell, 1994.

Neyrey, Jerome H. "Ceremonies in Luke-Acts: The Case of Meals and Table Fellowship." In Jerome H. Neyrey, ed., *The Social World of Luke-Acts: Models for Interpretation*. Peabody, MA: Hendrickson, 1991, 361–87.

―――. "Reader's Guide to Meals, Food and Table Fellowship in the New Testament," at www.nd.edu/~jneyrey1/meals/html.

Nielsen, Inge, and Hanne Sigismund Nielson, eds. *Meals in a Social Context: Aspects of the Communal Meal in the Hellenistic and Roman World*. Aarhus Studies in Mediterranean Antiquity 1. Aarhus: Aarhus University Press, 1998.

Resseguie, James L. *Spiritual Landscape: Images of the Spiritual Life in the Gospel of Luke*. Peabody, MA: Hendrickson, 2003.

Shapiro, Laura. *Something from the Oven: Reinventing Dinner in 1950s America*. New York: Viking, 2004.

Smith, Dennis E. *From Symposium to Eucharist: The Banquet in the Early Christian World*. Minneapolis: Fortress, 2003.

————. "Dinner with Jesus & Paul: The Social Role of Meals in the Greco-Roman World." *Bible Review* 20 (4) (August 2004) 30–39, 45.

Webster, Jane S. *Ingesting Jesus: Eating and Drinking in the Gospel of John.* Society of Biblical Literature Academia Biblica 6. Atlanta: Society of Biblical Literature, 2003.

Correlation of Pages in the Book with Readings of Luke's Gospel in Sunday Cycle C

This appendix consists of a correlation of pages in my book with passages in Luke's Gospel as these passages occur in the Roman Catholic Sunday Lectionary for Cycle C. I provide it as a refresher for those who have read my entire book and now, as they prepare a homily for liturgy, want to recall what I said about a specific passage. This aide should not be seen as a dispensation from reading an individual passage in its immediate and total context in Luke's Gospel. See pages 13–14 above.

Third Sunday of Advent (n. 9)
   Luke 3:10-18   See 26–30, esp. 29
Fourth Sunday of Advent (n. 12)
   Luke 1:39-45   See 83–84
Christmas; January 1
   (nn. 14-15, 18) Luke 2:1-20   See 16, 98, 100
4th Sunday of Lent (n. 33)
   Luke 15:1-32   See 59–60, 63
Palm Sunday (n. 38)
   Luke 22:14–23:56   See 31–32, 37–39,
                                        88–93, 99, 101

Easter (n. 42) Luke 24:13-35   See 48–50
Ascension (n. 58) Luke 24:46-53   See 93–94

Body and Blood of Christ (n. 169)
    Luke 9:11b-17   See 50–52, 98–99
5th Sunday in Ordinary Time (n. 75)
    Luke 5:1-11   See 7, 30–32
11th Sunday in Ordinary Time (n. 93)
    Luke 7:36–8:3   See 35–36, 42–44,
                                      85–87, 100

16th Sunday in Ordinary Time (n. 108)
    Luke 10:38-42   See 87–88, 100
17th Sunday in Ordinary Time (n. 111)
    Luke 11:1-13   See 55–56, 101
22nd Sunday in Ordinary Time (n. 126)
    Luke 14:1-14   See 46–48, 65
24th Sunday in Ordinary Time (n. 132)
    Luke 15:1-32   See 59–60, 63
26th Sunday in Ordinary Time (n. 138)
    Luke 16:19-31   See 63–64, 92–93
31st Sunday in Ordinary Time (n. 153)
    Luke 19:1-10   See 36–37
Christ the King (n. 162)
    Luke 23:35-43   See 37–39

Index

Abraham, 37
Ambrose, Saint, 38
Animals, 21–23
Apuleius, 10, 42

Babette's Feast, 98, 103
Barber, Samuel, 101
Bauckham, Richard, 87, 95
Bonaventure, St., 21, 24, 46, 49, 53
Boat for fishing, 7, 30
Braun, Willi, 46, 54
Bread, 7–8, 102
Brigit, St., 101
Broshi, Magen, 6–7, 11

Catholic Theological Union, 1
Cato, 6
Co, Maria Anicia, 86, 95

Dalby, Andrew, 5, 7, 11
Deuteronomy 21:18-21, 26–27
Dodd, C. H., 55

Elizabeth, 83–84
Eucharist, 13–14, 48–50, 52, 88–93
Extraordinary event, 43, 45

Firmage, Edwin, 5, 11
Fish, 7, 30
Franciscan School of Theology, 2
Friend, 27–28

Gibson, Mel, 37
Good Thief, 37–39
Graduate Theological Union, 1
Grassi, Joseph, 21, 24
Gregory the Great, St., 38

Hamel, Gildas, 5, 12
Hanson, K. C., 7, 12
"Hermit Songs," 101
Hospitality, 9–10
Hultgren, Arland J., 62

Jeremias, Joachim, 32–33
Jesus, 97–99
Jesus' disciples, 99–102
Jewell, Jack, 98
Joanna, 85–87
Jung, L. Shannon, 101–3
Junia, 82
Juvenal, 8

Karris, Robert J., 1, 24, 54, 65, 96

Lazarus, 15, 63–64, 92–93
Lectionary, RC, 13, 106–7
Lectionary-itis, 13
Leonardo da Vinci, 90
Levi, 32–34
Lucian of Samosata, 9, 43
Luke, Gospel of
    1:39-56, 83–84
    2:7, 98
    3:11, 13
    5:1-11, 30–31
    5:27-32, 32–34
    7:34, 26–30
    7:36-50, 35–36, 42–44
    8:1-3, 85–87
    9:10-17, 50–52
    10:38-42, 87–88
    11:3, 55–56
    11:37-54, 44–46
    12:35-40, 60
    13:18-21, 60–62
    14:1-14, 46–48
    14:15-24, 63
    15:4-7, 63
    16:19-31, 63–64
    19:1-10, 36–37
    22:14-38, 88–93
    22:31-34, 54-62, 31–32
    23:39-43, 37–39
    24:13-35, 48–50
    24:34-42, 31–32
    24:36-52, 93–94

Magnificat, 64, 84
Martha and Mary, 87–88
Mary of Magdala, 7, 83, 85–87
Mary of Nazareth, 83–84
McBain, Ed, 42
Meat, 5

Moloney, Francis J., 101, 103
Oakman, Douglas E., 7, 12
Ovid, 10

Parables in Luke, 56–64
Paradise, 38–39
Peter, 30–32
Pliny the Elder, 61
Plutarch, 9, 47
Proverbs 23:20-21, 26–27

Recipe for beer bread, 56
Revelation 2:7, 38

Sawicki, Marianne, 86, 96
Sinners, 29–30
Sirach 13:13-19, 27
Seutonius, 100
Susanna, 85–87
Symposium, 8–9, 20–21

Testament of Levi, 38–39
The Da Vinci Code, 35
Theme, detecting a, 14–15
Theme of food in John, 66–70
Theme of food in Mark, 70–74
Theme of food in Matthew, 74–80
Theme of food in Luke, 16–21
Toll collectors, 28–29

Vitellius, Emperor, 100
Vööbus, Arthur, 92

Water, 5–6
Webb, Stephen H., 99, 103
Webster, Jane S., 14–15, 24, 69, 81, 106
Wine, 6
Women, 82–93

Zacchaeus, 36–37